... when you need it in writing!™

PERSONNEL DIRECTOR®

Over 240 ready-to-use personnel agreements... forms... letters... and documents to manage your employees more efficiently, effectively... and legally!

compiled by
Sondra Servais

E-Z LEGAL BOOKS®

384 South Military Trail, Deerfield Beach, Florida 33442
phone: (305) 480-8933 • (800) 822-4566 • fax: (305) 480-8906

... when you need it in writing! ®

E-Z Legal Forms, Inc.
384 S. Military Trail
Deerfield Beach FL 33442

Distributed by E-Z Legal Forms, Inc.

Manufactured in the United States of America

1 2 3 4 5 6 7 8 9 10

This book is sold with the understanding that neither the author nor the publisher is engaged in rendering legal advice. If legal advice is required, the services of an attorney should be sought. Publisher and author cannot in any way guarantee that the forms in this book are being used for the purposes intended and, therefore, assume no responsibility for their proper and correct use.

Library of Congress Catalog Card Number: 94-070367

Personnel Director
  Compiled by Sondra Servais.
      p.   cm.
  ISBN 1-56382-302-0: $24.95
I. Servais, Sondra, compiled by. II. Title: Personnel Director

IMPORTANT FACTS

E-Z Legal Products are designed to provide authoritative and accurate information in regard to the subject matter covered. However, neither this nor any other publication can take the place of an attorney on important legal matters.

Information in this book has been carefully compiled from sources believed to be reliable, but the accuracy of the information is not guaranteed, as laws and regulations may change or be subject to differing interpretations.

Why not have your attorney review this book? We encourage it.

E-Z LEGAL FORMS
384 S. Military Trail
Deerfield Beach, FL 33442
Tel. 305-480-8933   Fax 305-480-8906

About Personnel Director...

Personnel Director contains all the important and ready-to-complete forms and documents you need to manage your company's people.

Virtually every personnel record-keeping form is at your fingertips, giving you the protection you need without the inconvenience or cost of using an attorney for simple personnel matters you can easily handle yourself.

E-Z Legal Forms' *Personnel Director* is the ideal way to "get it in writing." What better way to legally document your important personnel agreements and contracts, avoid troublesome disputes, enforce your legal rights, comply with legal obligations and avoid liability?

Virtually every size and type of business can use *Personnel Director*. It can be used by both non-profit and profit businesses to document employee turnover, agreements, payroll and policies. It will be particularly useful to time-starved small and mid-sized businesses, which can easily keep up-to-date, accurate and valuable personnel records with this book.

Written by a panel of attorneys and law professors, *Personnel Director* can be used with confidence by non-lawyers.

How to Use Personnel Director

You can easily and conveniently use *Personnel Director* by following these simple instructions.

1 To find the appropriate form, you can check the Table of Contents. Each entry contains a cross-reference to our *Personnel Director* software.

2 You may find several forms for the same general purpose, so review and select the form most appropriate for your specific needs.

3 Each form is perforated for easy removal and use. Photocopy and store the original so it can be used again and again.

4 Fully complete each form. Make certain all blanks (name, address, dates, amounts) are filled in. Delete, modify or add provisions as required. Attach a separate addendum if additional terms cannot be easily inserted. All changes or addendums should be initialed by all parties. Verbal terms are generally not enforceable, so make certain your document includes all that was agreed upon.

5 Correspondence forms can be personalized by reproducing on your letterhead. You may want to obliterate form numbers and page numbers at bottom of pages, and in some cases remove the form name from the top.

6 Read the material that precedes each section for a description of each form.

7 The pronoun "it" within a form can properly refer to an individual as well as a business entity.

8 Important correspondence should always be delivered by certified mail, return receipt requested.

9 Use caution and common sense when using E-Z Legal Forms — or any other do-it-yourself legal product. While these forms are generally considered appropriate for self-use, you must nevertheless decide when you should instead seek professional legal advice. You should certainly consult an attorney when:

- You need a complex or important agreement.
- Your transaction involves large amounts of money or expensive property.
- You don't understand how to use a document — or question its adequacy to fully protect you.

Because we cannot be certain that the forms in this book are appropriate to your circumstances — or are being properly used — we cannot assume any liability or responsibility in connection with their use.

Table of Contents

Section 2

Section 3

Section 4

Section 5

Section 6

Section 7

Why you need Personnel Director

Personnel Director can save you both time and money in the administration of your business, so you can spend more time running your business profitably, efficiently and without costly legal problems.

Personnel Director also gives your business a professional approach to handling the numerous tasks of dealing with employees.

Whatever size or type of business you operate, and no matter how effective your present personnel management program, the forms in *Personnel Director* can help make your business more successful.

Personnel Director is now used by thousands of businesses of every size and type to improve personnel management, increase employee productivity and reduce liability.

Personnel Director can help you:

- Attract and retain the most qualified employees.

- Spend less time orienting new employees and supervising present personnel.

- Accurately and objectively evaluate personnel performance.

- Increase productivity, goodwill and morale.

- Document and streamline every phase of your personnel management program for peak performance.

- Reduce or avoid expensive legal fees in preparing important contracts and agreements.

- Comply with state and federal employment law.

- Insulate your business from costly employee lawsuits.

Personnel Director guides you through every stage of managing employees — from recruiting and hiring to discharges and termination. *Personnel Director* not only gives you a more sensible, professionally prepared personnel program but also saves you time and money in managing your organization's most valuable asset — its people.

Recruiting and Hiring

Without a doubt, the most important and time-consuming aspect of any business today is finding the right people to help you run it. *Personnel Director* provides you with the ready-to-complete forms to make this part of the process much less time consuming. From posting a job opening to scheduling interviews to verifying an applicant's background, all the forms you need to conduct your search and organize the information you need to make a hiring decision are right here.

This section also contains application forms, authorizations, correspondence and rating summaries to help streamline decision-making and communication with applicants and references. Responding to applicants will be a breeze with *Personnel Director*, which includes acknowledgements of resumes and references, requests for information and verification, and replies to applicants who interview for a position but are not hired.

Other forms in this section can help you set up programs for employee referral (Bonus for Employee Referral, Employee Referral Request, Prospective Employee Referral, Applicant Referral Program) or in-house recruitment (Job Bid, Notice of Available Position), identify handicapped or veteran applicants or protect yourself from costly claims of discriminatory hiring practices (Employment Application Disclaimer and Acknowledgement, Applicant Waiver).

Employment Agreements

Personnel Director contains more than 20 agreements for a variety of situations to safeguard a company's interests. Independent Contractor's Agreement or Acknowledgements of Temporary Employment clearly establish your relationship with a contractor or temporary employee and avoid future potentially costly claims of an employer/employee relationship. Sales Representative Agreements define a sales rep's obligations to the company. Employee Agreements should be used when filling any professional, technical or managerial position within your company. *Personnel Director* also includes additional forms to extend, modify or change these agreements.

Protecting your patents, inventions and trade secrets may be the most important thing you can do to ensure your company's continued existence. Similarly, confidentiality and non-compete agreements and covenants safeguard your company from former employees using their knowledge to lure customers and accounts away from you.

Ready-to-complete waivers and indemnities help you avoid liability. Recover expenses reimbursed to employees if the IRS disallows them as deductions. Obtain employees' consent for drug, alcohol and polygraph testing. Ensure that your employees refrain from involvement in any activity in conflict with your business. And prevent an employee from suing you for changing his schedule.

Processing New Employees

This area of personnel management can involve the most paperwork. *Personnel Director* can simplify your work by providing ready-to-use forms for new employees to complete and sign. Letters to new employees confirm start dates and times. The New Employee Announcement provides a quick and convenient vehicle for notifying others in your company about new personnel, who they are, their background and experience.

Information on withholding tax, payroll deductions, direct deposits, an employee's background and emergency phone numbers can be obtained conveniently in one session. Use these documents to prepare an Employee File. Provide your new employees with a Job Description, outlines of Emergency Procedures, Employee Agreement, Handbook Acknowledgement and a Summary of Employment Terms the minute they arrive for their first day on the job.

Be prepared to introduce them to your company with an Orientation Checklist. Have them sign for company property and/or samples and documents as they are issued. Then use the EEO Analysis of New Hires to see where your company stands in hiring minorities and women.

Personnel Management

Under the broad umbrella of personnel management falls scheduling, payroll and record keeping. Whether you have one or several dozen employees, keeping track of when they work; how much they get paid; or when they are absent, injured or sick can be a time-consuming task. *Personnel Director* can help ease your burden.

This section contains the perfect form to record an employee's history with the company, make changes to an employee's file or salary record or verify the accuracy of information you have on an employee. You can also implement a program for employees to inspect their personnel files and keep a record of access to those files.

Providing references to banks, mortgage companies and car dealerships concerning your employees can be a snap with *Personnel Director*. Be sure to obtain consent from your employees to release such information.

Keep track of employee turnover and projected personnel needs with the Personnel Activity Report and Personnel Requirements Projections. Document your temporary employment needs.

Setting schedules was never easier with the Employee Flextime and Weekly Work schedules. Keep a record of time worked daily and weekly, and keep a watchful eye on overtime with *Personnel Director's* request, permit, authorization and follow-up procedure for overtime. Simplify vacation planning using the Vacation Request and Vacation Request Memo.

Accident, illness and injury reports can be invaluable tools for pointing out areas in the workplace that require improvement. They can also pinpoint the need to certify an employee's disability or illness if frequent absences occur. This process can protect you from erroneous disability claims.

Personnel Director also contains sample Employee Suggestion Plans that you can adopt or custom-design. A host of affirmative action notices, policies and analyses help you tell others about your commitment to equal opportunity employment as well as identify those areas of your personnel management program that may need improvement.

You can also find an Employee Transfer Request, an Off-Duty Employment Request and a Grievance Form in this section.

Performance Evaluation

An ongoing program of performance evaluation provides the key to improving an employee's value to your company. *Personnel Director* makes it easy to implement and follow through with an evaluation program. Whether reviewing an employee's performance for a salary increase or determining the need for stronger disciplinary action, you will find the form you need in this section.

When problems occur with an employee who is habitually late or absent or has difficulty following company policy, *Personnel Director* offers an ironclad process of documentation and an increasingly strict set of disciplinary steps designed to correct the problem. Notices, warnings, consultations and counseling can precede any final termination action. Following these steps with *Personnel Director* will give you adequate legal protection should an employee claim unfair employment practices or discrimination.

New employees are given a job description upon beginning employment and know what is expected of them. Goals and objectives for each employee are set and later reviewed for performance.

Weaknesses and strengths are identified and areas for improvement are discussed. Employees can rate their own accomplishments and respond to a supervisor's comments. These are reviewed to set new goals and objectives for the next evaluation.

You may find an employee deserving of a letter of commendation or a raise! Let *Personnel Director* help you recognize those occasions.

Benefits

Benefits go hand in hand with personnel management. *Personnel Director* gives you the tools you need to survey employees about the benefits they would like and to compare your current benefit offerings with a competitor's.

In addition, you will find it easy to add to your basic benefits list a number of special benefits that your company can adopt by resolution. From a signing bonus to entice a prospective employee to join your company to implementing a child care plan for your employees, you can make your company stand out from the crowd in the way of benefits when you have *Personnel Director* at your side.

Provide your employees with a merchandise discount program, financial counseling, tuition benefits or scholarship aid. Wage continuation plans and low-interest loan programs are great benefits to attract and keep employees. For those key employees, you can offer an at-home entertainment allowance, a company car, club membership, paid-up annuity or stock-option plan.

A sabbatical leave could be the ideal benefit to entice a long-term important employee to stay on. A relocation allowance may be the answer for a prospective employee to accept your job offer, and performance bonuses go a long way to reward hard-working, loyal employees.

Periodically, you may want to remind your employees of the value of their benefits. The Accrued Benefits Statement is perfect for summing up what your company does for its employees.

Separation and Termination

Terminating employees is never easy. But *Personnel Director* keeps you one step ahead with a handy checklist of items to complete during the process. You will find the ideal termination letter among the variety included in this book, from termination due to absence to reduction in workforce to intoxication on the job.

Not all separations are due to termination. *Personnel Director* also includes a Retirement Checklist and a Resignation. The Employee Checkout Record will help you remember all those little details, such as keys, credit cards or supplies to be returned. It is always a good idea to have exiting employees sign some kind of release, whether it is mutual, general or solely on the part of the employee. This could protect you from any perceived legal claims by a disgruntled former employee.

The Employee Exit Interview can be an invaluable tool for identifying problem areas in the company. The Separation Notice, Personnel Separation Report and Employee Separation Report detail the circumstances leading up to a separation and become part of the former employee's file. This will help when you receive requests for references from other employers. *Personnel Director* also includes forms that make responding to requests for references easy, such as Reference Report, Employment Reference Response and Refusal to Grant References.

The Notice of Confidentiality Agreement informs a new employer that you expect a confidentiality agreement between you and a former employee to be honored.

Record keeping and paperwork continue right through termination and beyond; the Consolidated Omnibus Budget Reconciliation Act of 1985 saw to that. This act provides terminated employees with continued medical insurance coverage at their expense (and your time) if they choose to enroll. *Personnel Director* provides forms to keep this paperwork accurate and under control. An Unemployment Compensation Record also helps you keep track of former employees who file unemployment claims.

Personnel Director can be your strongest organizational tool for personnel management, whether you have a program in place or are looking to implement one. Don't be left behind in a pile of personnel paperwork. Let *Personnel Director* take some of the burden off your shoulders so you can spend more time making your business grow!

Section 1
Recruiting and Hiring

Form N101   **Notice of Available Position** – Lists duties and qualifications for employment opening.

Form H101   **Help Wanted Advertising Listing** – Records information for placing an advertisement to fill a job opening.

Form B101   **Bonus for Employee Referral** – Letter notifying employee of earning a bonus for referring an applicant who was hired by the company.

Form E101   **Employee Referral Request** – Letter notifying employees of bonus program for referring applicants.

Form P101   **Prospective Employee Referral** – Form used by employee to refer prospective employee to company.

Form A101   **Applicant Referral Program** – Response from company to employee regarding referral.

Form J101   **Job Bid** – Records current employee's interest in another position within company.

Form R101   **Resume Acknowledgement** – Letter acknowledging receipt of resume.

Form A102   **Applicant Acknowledgement Letter** – Acknowledges applicant's response to advertisement for position.

Form A103   **Acknowledgement of Reference** – Letter acknowledging receipt of reference from another company.

Form A104   **Applicant Interview Confirmation Letter** – Confirms date and time of applicant's scheduled interview.

Form P102   **Preliminary Employment Application** – A brief record of applicant's employment goals and history.

Form V101   **Veteran/Handicapped Status** – Records the handicapped and/or veteran status of an applicant.

Form E102   **Employment Application** – Detailed record of applicant's employment history, skills and education.

Form E103   **Employment Application Disclaimer and Acknowledgement** – Attests to correctness of application and authorizes release of information.

Form A105   **Applicant Waiver** – Certifies the accuracy of an application and acknowledges no guarantee of employment.

Form A106   **Authorization to Release Information** – Authorizes the release of education, military and employment information.

Form M101   **Medical Testing Authorization** – Grants authority to perform specific medical tests and releases company from any responsibility.

Form A107   **Applicant Interview Schedule** – Lists dates and times of interviews scheduled for various positions.

Form R102   **Reschedule Appointment Letter** – Notifies applicant of change in appointment.

Form I101   **Interviewing Checklist** – Highlights questions to avoid asking candidates for employment and promotion.

Form A108   **Applicant Rating** – Rates an individual applicant on job requirements.

Form C101   **Clerical Applicant Rating** – Rates an individual applicant's office skills.

Form J102   **Job Applicant Rating** – Rates an individual's education, experience, interpersonal and communication skills.

Form A109   **Applicant Interview Summary** – Summarizes an applicant's impressions on and responses to an interviewer's questions.

Form A110   **Applicant Comparison Summary** – Compares the job requirements ratings of three candidates.

Form T101   **Telephone Reference Checklist** – Records reference responses to questions regarding a specific applicant.

Form M102   **Medical Records Request** – Requests the release of medical information.

Form R103   **Request for Reference** – Requests employment information from previous employer.

Form R104   **Request for Transcript** – Requests a copy of school grades and attendance record.

Form V102   **Verification of Education** – Verifies an applicant's education record.

Form V103   **Verification of Employment** – Verifies an applicant's employment record.

Form V104   **Verification of Licensure** – Verifies an applicant's license or registration with the state.

Form V105   **Verification of Military Status** – Verifies an applicant's military record.

Form U101   **Unsuccessful Candidate Letter** – Letter rejecting an applicant for hire.

Form A111   **Applicant Rejection Letter 1** – Letter rejecting an applicant for hire.

Form A112   **Applicant Rejection Letter 2** – Letter rejecting an applicant for hire.

Form A113   **Applicant Letter** – Letter requesting applicant to contact company to discuss job opening.

Form A114   **Applicant Reply Letter** – Response to applicant's inquiry regarding employment opportunities.

Form N102   **No Decision on Hiring Letter** – Letter informing applicant of company's indecision to fill position.

Form E104   **Employment Confirmation Letter** – Confirms acceptance of employment offer with successful candidate.

NOTICE OF AVAILABLE POSITION

Starting Date: _____ Date Posted: _____

Position: _____

Description Of Duties:

Qualifications Required:

Salary:

Contact:

We are an Affirmative Action/Equal Opportunity Employer

HELP WANTED ADVERTISING LISTING

Position: _____ Req. #: _____

Department/Division: _____

Charge to: _____ (Department)

Person Requesting Ad: _____ Phone Ext.: _____

Newspaper: _____

Run Ad: _____ (days) _____(dates)

Under Classified Heading: _____

Please insert the following ad:

For Department Use Only

Ad Placed:_____ (date) _____(newspaper)

Cost: $ _____

Ad To Run: _____ (days) _____(dates)

Re-Run Ordered: _____ (date) _____(newspaper)

Re-Run Cost: $ _____

Responses

_____

_____

_____

_____

 FORM H101

BONUS FOR EMPLOYEE REFERRAL

Date:

To:

The individual you referred for consideration for employment has been hired and has completed _____ months of service. Enclosed you will find, as provided in our policy manual, a check for $_____ as a "thank you" for the referral.

Your efforts in finding quality recruits for employment are truly appreciated.

Sincerely,

_____
Personnel Manager

EMPLOYEE REFERRAL REQUEST

Date:

To:

     We consider our employees to be an excellent source for locating other qualified prospective employees.

     Please refer individuals known to you who are qualified for any existing or potential vacancy to the undersigned.

     Our "employee through employee" candidate referral program is a valuable tool to bring in quality recruits, and to build goodwill among present employees. In addition, as an incentive, for each referral who is subsequently hired and remains with us for a period of _____ months, the referring employee will receive $_____.

     Thank you for your efforts.

Sincerely,

_____
Personnel Manager

FORM E101

PROSPECTIVE EMPLOYEE REFERRAL

Referring Employee:_____

Employee #: _____ Department:_____

Individual Referred: _____

Address: _____

For (specify position):_____

Years Known: _____ Relationship to Employee:_____

Qualifications

_____

_____

_____

_____

_____

_____

_____

Other Comments in Support of Prospective Employee

_____

_____

_____

_____

_____

_____

_____

_____

Employee Signature:_____

APPLICANT REFERRAL PROGRAM

To:

Date:

From:

Thank you for your recent referral of
for the position of   .

The status of this candidate is:

_____ No longer interested in employment.

_____ Job was offered and declined.

_____ Job offer is pending.

_____ Currently being interviewed.

_____ Resume on file; no current openings.

_____ Not qualified.

Thank you for your support and participation in the employee referral program. If any further action is taken regarding this candidate, we will notify you.

_____
Personnel Manager

FORM A101

JOB BID

Employee: _____ Date: _____

Current Department: _____

Current Supervisor: _____

Position Applying For: _____ Dept.:_____

Qualifications for the Job: _____

_____

_____

_____

Other Qualifications (degrees, licenses, etc.): _____

_____

_____

_____

_____

Employee Signature

For Department Use Only

Date Employee Interviewed _____

Did Employee Get the Job? _____ Yes _____ No

If Not, Why Not?_____

_____

Has Employee's Supervisor Been Notified? _____

Has Employee Been Notified? _____

_____

Department Representative

RESUME ACKNOWLEDGEMENT

Date:

To:

Thank you for your correspondence and resume concerning a position with our firm.

We do want to inform you that your information is being reviewed for employment consideration. We will contact you for an interview if your qualifications meet our current needs.

We appreciate your interest in our firm.

Sincerely,

_____

Personnel Manager

APPLICANT ACKNOWLEDGEMENT

Date:

To:

Thank you for responding to our advertisement for the position of

.

Your qualifications, as communicated in your letter and resume, appear to meet the minimum requirements for the position. As scheduling permits, we would like to arrange for an interview at our offices located at

.

Please call   at
to make an appointment for your interview.

Thank you for your interest in the above position.

Sincerely,

_____

Personnel Manager

ACKNOWLEDGEMENT OF REFERENCE

Date:

To:

Re:

Dear   :

Thank you for your reference on the above individual. The applicant (   ) was (   ) was not offered a position with our firm, and your appraisal of the applicant's performance while employed with your firm was certainly an important factor in our decision.

We will hold your reference confidential unless you have authorized disclosure, and once again, we thank you for your cooperation, and would be pleased to reciprocate the courtesy.

Very truly,

_____
Title

FORM A103

APPLICANT INTERVIEW CONFIRMATION

Date:

To:

This will confirm your appointment for an interview for the position of
. The interview will be at our offices
located at   at   m. You can
expect the interview to take approximately   hours.

You will first meet with   , the
. You are scheduled to meet later
with   .

After the interview, we will contact you regarding our decision.

Once again, thank you for your interest in our firm. We look forward to seeing you
on the above date.

Sincerely,

_____

Personnel Manager

PRELIMINARY EMPLOYMENT APPLICATION

I understand that this is not a full application. I understand this application will be reviewed and my qualifications considered for possible job openings in the future.

Name: _____ Date: _____

Address: _____ City: _____

State: _____ Zip: _____ Phone: _____

Position Desired: _____ Requested Wages: $ _____ per _____

TYPE OF EMPLOYMENT

❑ Seasonal ❑ Temporary ❑ Permanent ❑ Full Time ❑ Part Time

Days available: ❑ Monday through Friday   ❑ Other (explain) _____

_____. Hours available: _____ to _____

EMPLOYMENT

Most recent or previous employer: _____

Dates Employed: _____ to: _____ Wages: $ _____ per_____

Describe Position & Duties:_____

EDUCATION

Enter the number of years completed:

High School: _____ Undergraduate College:_____ Graduate/Professional School:_____

Describe your major areas of studies: _____

_____

Other training: _____

List other information for the employment you are seeking: _____

_____

All potential employees are evaluated without regard to race, color, religion, gender, national origin, age, marital or veteran status, the presence of a non-job related handicap or any other legally protected status.

Signature:_____ Date:_____

Print Name:_____

FORM P102

VETERAN/HANDICAPPED STATUS

Applicant: _____

Position Sought:_____

    Federal regulations require that employers take affirmative action to provide equal employment opportunity for the handicapped and Vietnam-era and disabled veterans.

    If you qualify and wish to be considered for these purposes, please check the appropriate box. It would assist us if you tell us about (1) any special methods, skills, or procedures that qualify you for positions you might not otherwise be able to do because of your handicap or disability, and (2) any accommodations we could make to assist you in performing the job properly and safely, including special equipment, changes in the physical layout of the job or elimination of certain duties relating to the job.

    Providing this confidential information is strictly voluntary. Refusal to provide it will not subject you to any adverse treatment. Any information provided will be used only in accordance with applicable federal laws and regulations.

Veteran/Handicapped Status:

_____	Disabled Veteran:	Any veteran entitled to disability compensation under the laws administered by the Veterans Administration for a disability rated at 30% or more, or any veteran discharged or released from active duty because of a disability incurred or aggravated in the line of duty.
_____	Vietnam-Era Veteran:	Any person who served in the military for more than 180 continuous days, any part of which occurred between Aug. 5, 1964, and May 7, 1975, and was discharged or released therefrom with other than a dishonorable discharge; or was discharged or released from active duty for a service-connected disability.
_____	Handicapped:	An person who has a physical or mental impairment that substantially limits such person's major life activities and that affects employability, has a record of having such an impairment, or is regarded as having such an impairment.

_____   _____
Applicant's signature   Date

EMPLOYMENT APPLICATION
(please print)

Full Name: _____

Address: _____

City: _____ State: _____ Zip: _____

Phone: _____ Social Security No: _____

Position Applied For: _____

Are you a citizen of the United States? ☐ Yes ☐ No

If not, do you have work papers? _____

Are you a veteran? _____ Yes _____ No Branch of Service: _____

EDUCATION
(name and location of school)

High School: _____

Did you graduate? _____ Degree: _____

Bus./Trade: _____

Did you graduate? _____ Degree: _____

Col./Univ.: _____

Did you graduate? _____ Degree: _____

Grad./Prof.: _____

Did you graduate? _____ Degree: _____

PREVIOUS EMPLOYMENT
(begin with most recent position)

Most recent

Firm:_____ Address: _____

Supervisor: _____ Nature of Business:_____

Dates of Employment:_____ Position(s) Held: _____

Ending Salary: _____ Reason for Leaving: _____

Previous Employer

Firm:_____ Address: _____

Supervisor: _____ Nature of Business:_____

Dates of Employment:_____ Position(s) Held: _____

Ending Salary: _____ Reason for Leaving: _____

FORM E102

Previous Employer

Firm: _____ Address: _____

Supervisor: _____ Nature of Business: _____

Dates of employment: _____ Position(s) Held: _____

Ending Salary: _____ Reason for Leaving: _____

REFERENCES

Please furnish the names and addresses of two people to whom you are not related and by whom you have not been employed.

Name: _____

Address: _____

Name: _____

Address: _____

Who referred you to us? (person or agency): _____

_____

Summarize your special skills or qualifications:

_____

_____

_____

I certify that my answers are true and complete to the best of my knowledge.

I authorize you to make such investigations and inquiries of my personal, employment, educational, financial, or medical history and other related matters as may be necessary for an employment decision. I hereby release employers, schools, or persons from all liability in responding to inquiries in connection with my application.

In the event I am employed, I understand that false or misleading information given in my application or interview(s) may result in discharge.

Signature of Applicant: _____ Date: _____

For Department Use Only

Action:_____

_____

_____

_____

EMPLOYMENT APPLICATION DISCLAIMER
AND ACKNOWLEDGEMENT

I certify that the information contained in this application is correct to the best of my knowledge. I understand that to falsify information is grounds for refusing to hire me, or for discharge should I be hired.

I authorize any person, organization or company listed on this application to furnish you any and all information concerning my previous employment, education and qualifications for employment. I also authorize you to request and receive such information.

In consideration for my employment, I agree to abide by the rules and regulations of the company, which rules may be changed, withdrawn, added or interpreted at any time, at the company's sole option and without prior notice to me.

I also acknowledge that my employment may be terminated, or any offer or acceptance of employment withdrawn, at any time, with or without cause, and with or without prior notice at the option of the company or myself.

Signature:_____   Date: _____

FORM E103

APPLICANT WAIVER
(All job applicants must sign and submit with application form)

I hereby certify that the information hereunder is correct to the best of my knowledge and understand that falsification of this information is grounds for refusal to hire or, if hired, dismissal.

I hereby authorize any of the persons or organizations listed in my application to give all information concerning my previous employment, education, or any other information they might have, personal or otherwise, with regard to any of the subjects covered by this application, and release all such parties from all liability that may result from furnishing such information to you. I authorize you to request and receive such information.

In consideration for my employment and my being considered for employment by your company, I agree to adhere to the rules and regulations of the company and hereby acknowledge that these rules and regulations may be changed by your company at any time, at the company's sole option and without any prior notice. In addition, I acknowledge that my employment may be terminated, and any offer of employment, if such is made, may be withdrawn, with or without prior notice, at any time, at the option of either the company or myself.

I understand that no representative of the company has any authority to enter into any agreement for employment for any specified period of time, or assure or make some other personnel move, either prior to commencement of employment or after I have become employed, or to assure any benefits or terms and conditions of employment, or make any agreement contrary to the foregoing.

I hereby acknowledge that I have been advised that this application will remain active for no more than 90 days from the date it was signed.

Applicant: _____   Date: _____

Company
Representative: _____   Date: _____

AUTHORIZATION TO RELEASE INFORMATION

To:

      Please be advised that I have applied for a position with
                   . I have been requested to provide
information for their use in reviewing my background and qualifications. Therefore, I
authorize the investigation of my past and present health, character, education, military
and employment qualifications.

      The release in any manner of all information by you is hereby authorized whether
such information is of record or not, and I do hereby release all persons, agencies or firms
from any liabilities resulting from providing such information.

      This authorization is valid for   days from the date of my signature below.
Please keep this copy of my release request for your files. Thank you for your cooperation.

Signature:_____   Date: _____

Witness: _____   Date: _____

FORM A106

MEDICAL TESTING AUTHORIZATION

I, the undersigned, declare that I am a competent adult at least 18 years old. I hereby grant permission for the following medical test to be performed on me:

I further acknowledge that such tests may involve the temporary invasion or penetration of my body by medical instruments, light, sound, x-rays, or other imaging and diagnostic media, and may further involve the obtainment of bodily fluids, tissue, products or waste, all of which I give up any claim to.

I further certify that all such contemplated tests have been explained to me and that I have provided complete and honest responses to all questions posed to me regarding my health, including pregnancy, disabilities, allergies, and susceptibilities, if any.

I understand that these medical tests are not being performed for my benefit, but are instead performed for the benefit of   ,
which I hereby release from any and all responsibility for treatment, advice, referral, or diagnosis.

I grant this authorization in exchange for the opportunity to be considered for employment, or for advancement in employment, or because such testing is required by law, and I acknowledge such testing is necessary and relevant to my employment.

I voluntarily make this grant without reservation.

_____   _____
Applicant   Date

_____   _____
Witness   Date

APPLICANT INTERVIEW SCHEDULE

Date: _____ Time: _____

Applicant: _____ Position: _____

Comments: _____

_____

Date: _____ Time: _____

Applicant: _____ Position: _____

Comments: _____

_____

Date: _____ Time: _____

Applicant: _____ Position: _____

Comments: _____

_____

Date: _____ Time: _____

Applicant: _____ Position: _____

Comments: _____

_____

Date: _____ Time: _____

Applicant: _____ Position: _____

Comments: _____

_____

FORM A107

RESCHEDULED APPOINTMENT

Date:

To:

Dear   :

    Your appointment with   on
at   m. has been rescheduled.

    Please accept our apologies for any inconvenience this may cause you.

    Your new appointment is scheduled for   m. on   .
If you are unable to make this appointment, please call   at
                to reschedule.

    We look forward to meeting with you then.

                Sincerely,

                _____
                Personnel Manager

INTERVIEWING CHECKLIST

Candidates for Employment:

Beware asking the following questions of an applicant before being hired:

- Date of birth
- Maiden name
- Previous married name
- Marital status
- Name of spouse
- Spouse's occupation and length of time on the job
- Spouse's place of employment
- Number of children and their ages
- Arrest record
- Convictions may be asked about, but you may not refuse employment before conviction unless it is a bona fide job qualification
- Whether child care has been arranged for the children
- Reasons which would prevent an applicant from maintaining employment
- Ancestry
- National origin/race
- Age
- Sex
- Religion
- Affiliations with: a) communist party, b) union
- Garnishment of wages

This information can be obtained only after employment, and can have no bearing on employment decisions.

Candidates for Promotion:

The information listed above also serves no purpose in evaluating an employee's qualifications for promotion or transfer within the company. Discussions with the employee's current supervisor and review of the personnel records as to work performance and potential are far more valuable. Concentrate on the employee's qualifications, performance, and potential to meet the job needs.

FORM I101

APPLICANT RATING

Applicant: _____

Position/Department: _____

Interviewed by: _____ Date: _____

Job Requirements:	Excellent	Good	Fair	Poor	N/A
_____	_____	_____	_____	_____	_____
_____	_____	_____	_____	_____	_____
_____	_____	_____	_____	_____	_____
_____	_____	_____	_____	_____	_____
_____	_____	_____	_____	_____	_____
_____	_____	_____	_____	_____	_____
_____	_____	_____	_____	_____	_____
_____	_____	_____	_____	_____	_____
_____	_____	_____	_____	_____	_____
_____	_____	_____	_____	_____	_____

General Comments/Overall Appraisal: _____

_____

_____

_____

_____

_____

Recommendation: Hire (   )   Reject (   )   Other(   ) _____

CLERICAL APPLICANT RATING

Applicant: _____

Position/Department: _____

Interviewed by: _____ Date: _____

Office Skills:	Excellent	Good	Fair	Poor	N/A
Typing:	_____	_____	_____	_____	_____
Shorthand:	_____	_____	_____	_____	_____
Switchboard:	_____	_____	_____	_____	_____
P.C./Software:	_____	_____	_____	_____	_____
Telephone:	_____	_____	_____	_____	_____
Job Experience:	_____	_____	_____	_____	_____
Record of Job Success:	_____	_____	_____	_____	_____
Compatibility:	_____	_____	_____	_____	_____
Ability to Communicate:	_____	_____	_____	_____	_____
Ambition, Motivation:	_____	_____	_____	_____	_____
Other: _____	_____	_____	_____	_____	_____
Other: _____	_____	_____	_____	_____	_____

General Comments/Overall Appraisal:

_____

_____

_____

_____

_____

_____

_____

Recommendation: Hire (   )   Reject (   )   Other(   ) _____

FORM C101

JOB APPLICANT RATING

Applicant: _____

Position/Department: _____

Interviewed by: _____ Date: _____

	Excellent	Good	Fair	Poor	N/A
Education:	_____	_____	_____	_____	_____
Experience:	_____	_____	_____	_____	_____
Attention to Detail:	_____	_____	_____	_____	_____
Cooperation:	_____	_____	_____	_____	_____
Initiative:	_____	_____	_____	_____	_____
Integrity:	_____	_____	_____	_____	_____
Interpersonal Skills:	_____	_____	_____	_____	_____
Learning Ability:	_____	_____	_____	_____	_____
Stress Tolerance:	_____	_____	_____	_____	_____
Verbal Communication:	_____	_____	_____	_____	_____
Other: _____	_____	_____	_____	_____	_____
Other: _____	_____	_____	_____	_____	_____

General Comments/Overall Appraisal:

_____

_____

_____

_____

_____

_____

_____

Recommendation: Hire (   )   Reject (   )   Other(   ) _____

APPLICANT INTERVIEW SUMMARY

Applicant: _____ Phone: _____

Position/Department:_____

Interviewed by: _____ Date: _____

Available Starting Date: _____ Now Employed? _____

Salary Requested: _____

	Excellent	Good	Fair	Poor	N/A
Appearance:	_____	_____	_____	_____	_____
Experience:	_____	_____	_____	_____	_____
Education:	_____	_____	_____	_____	_____
Skills:	_____	_____	_____	_____	_____
Enthusiasm:	_____	_____	_____	_____	_____
Attitude:	_____	_____	_____	_____	_____
Other: _____	_____	_____	_____	_____	_____
Other: _____	_____	_____	_____	_____	_____

General Comments/Overall Appraisal:

_____

_____

_____

_____

_____

_____

_____

Recommendation: Hire ( )   Reject ( )   Other( ) _____

FORM A109

APPLICANT COMPARISON SUMMARY

Position: _____ Date: _____

Interviewer: _____

Candidate 1: _____

Candidate 2: _____

Candidate 3: _____

Legend:

✓   Meets job requirements
+   Exceeds job requirements
-    Does not meet job requirements

Job Requirements	1	2	3	Comments
_____	____	____	____	_____
_____	____	____	____	_____
_____	____	____	____	_____
_____	____	____	____	_____
_____	____	____	____	_____
_____	____	____	____	_____
_____	____	____	____	_____
_____	____	____	____	_____
_____	____	____	____	_____
_____	____	____	____	_____
_____	____	____	____	_____
_____	____	____	____	_____
_____	____	____	____	_____
_____	____	____	____	_____
_____	____	____	____	_____

TELEPHONE REFERENCE CHECKLIST

Applicant:_____

Position applied for: _____

Person contacted: _____

Telephone: _____

Title: _____ Company: _____

Address: _____

_____ has applied for a position with us.

Would you please verify the following information?

- Dates of employment: From _____To _____

- What was his or her position?

_____

_____

- Did he or she have supervisory responsibilities?

_____

_____

- How would you evaluate his or her work?

_____

_____

- Did the individual progress satisfactorily in the job?

_____

_____

- List his or her strong points.

_____

_____

- Were there any limitations?

_____

_____

FORM T101

MEDICAL RECORDS REQUEST

Date:

To:

Re: Social Security No.:

Dear   :

                                                            has applied to this company for

employment in the position of   .

    Because of the physical requirements this position entails, we request the following medical records:

    Please note the signature of the applicant granting permission below. Thank you for your cooperation.

Sincerely,

_____

I irrevocably authorize release of all requested medical information to the above-listed requesting company.

Applicant's
Signature:_____   Date: _____

REQUEST FOR REFERENCE

Date:

To:

Re:

    The above named individual has applied for a position with our company and indicates previous employment with your firm. The information requested below will help us to evaluate the applicant. We will hold your comments in strict confidence. Thank you for your cooperation.

Sincerely,

_____

Personnel Department

Please Indicate:

Position With Your Firm: _____

Employed From: _____ to _____

Final Salary: $ _____ Social Security No.:_____

Please rate the applicant on the basis of his or her employment with you (good/fair/poor):

Ability: _____ Conduct: _____ Attitude: _____

Efficiency: _____ Attendance:_____ Punctuality: _____

What was the reason for termination? _____

_____

Would you re-hire? _____. If not, give reason: _____

_____

_____

Signature and Title

REQUEST FOR TRANSCRIPT

Date:

To:

     Please be advised that I am being considered for employment by _____ and, in order to complete my application, they have requested a copy of my school transcript.

     Please send a transcript to the following:

       Firm: _____

       Address: _____

       _____

       Attention: _____

Thank you.

               Sincerely,

               _____

Attended: _____ to _____
            (month & year)   (month & year)

Degree/Diploma Received: _____

Enclosed is $_____ to cover cost of transcript.

VERIFICATION OF EDUCATION

Date:

To:

Re:

The above individual has applied to our organization for employment.

According to the information in the employment application, this individual has attended your school. Would you please verify the above by completing the following information?

Dates Attended:

Still Attending?

Degree/Diploma Earned:

Grade Point Average:

Honors or Commendations:

Other Comments:

Your cooperation in completing and returning this in the self-enclosed envelope is greatly appreciated.

Very truly,

_____

Personnel Manager

FORM V102

VERIFICATION OF EMPLOYMENT

Date:

Ref: (Applicant Name)

Dear   :

    The individual identified above is being evaluated for employment and has signed our employment application authorizing this inquiry. We would appreciate a statement of your experiences with this person when employed by your company. Please provide the information requested on the bottom of this letter and return to us in the enclosed self-addressed stamped envelope at your earliest convenience. Your reply will be held in strict confidence. We sincerely appreciate your cooperation and will gladly reciprocate.

Sincerely,

_____

CONFIDENTIAL

Applicant Name: _____

Address: _____

Name of Former Company: _____

Address: _____

Employed From _____ To _____

General Work Record: _____

_____

_____

_____

_____
Signed

VERIFICATION OF LICENSURE

Date:

To:

Please be advised that as a condition of my employment with
_____ , I hereby authorize release of information relative
to the status of my license or registration as a
within the State of   .

Please certify below and return to:

     Firm: _____

     Address: _____

     _____

     Attention: _____

Thank you.

                     Sincerely,

                    _____

CERTIFICATION

This will certify that the above,   , is
duly licensed in the State of   as a
and said license or registration is in good standing with no
disciplinary or revocation proceedings pending.

Dated: _____   _____
                              Certifying Official

FORM V104

VERIFICATION OF MILITARY STATUS

Date:

To:

Please be advised I am being considered for a position with

.

I am required to furnish them information for use in determining my eligibility.

Therefore, I hereby authorize release of the information below from my military and related medical records.

- ❑ Branch of Service _____
- ❑ Date separated from active service _____
- ❑ Service No. _____
- ❑ Type Discharge _____
- ❑ Present Military Status _____
- ❑ Social Security No. _____

Kindly furnish information to:

Firm: _____

Address: _____

_____

Attention: _____

_____
Signature of Applicant

Present Home Address

_____

_____

Date:

To:

Thank you for responding to our employment advertisement, and interviewing with us on   .

Your background and experience would certainly benefit many employers. However, we have selected another candidate who better meets our current requirements.

Thank you for your interest in the position and best wishes in your future endeavors.

Sincerely,

_____
Personnel Manager

Date:

To:

Dear   :

After careful deliberation, we have decided that another candidate for the position you applied for was closer to our job specifications.

This in no way reflects on the quality of your background or your character. Those in our company who interviewed you were impressed with your experience and background.

We wish you much luck in your career, confident that you will be an asset to another company. We sincerely regret it couldn't be with ours.

Sincerely,

_____

Personnel Manager

Date:

To:

Dear   :

Thank you for your inquiry on our recent advertisement for the position of
.

We appreciate the opportunity to review your credentials and were pleased that you are interested in employment with us.

We have narrowed our search to those few applicants who have the specific qualifications and experience we need for this position. Although your credentials do not specifically meet our current needs, we will retain your resume for six months in the event that an appropriate opportunity matching your background becomes available.

Thank you again for your interest, and we wish you the best of luck in your employment search.

Sincerely,

_____
Personnel Manager

APPLICANT REJECTION LETTER 2 – FORM A112

APPLICANT NOTIFICATION

Date:

To:

Dear   :

    I am in receipt of your letter and resume in response to our ad for a
position. Thank you for your interest in our firm.

    We have been unsuccessful in our attempts to reach you by phone.

    I would be willing to discuss our job opening with you if you contact me at your
earliest convenience at this telephone number:

    I look forward to hearing from you.

            Sincerely,

_____

APPLICANT REPLY

Date:

To:

Dear   :

     Thank you for your inquiry regarding employment opportunities with our company.

Unfortunately, we do not anticipate any openings for
                             at the time you expect to graduate. However, we
will retain the information you submitted for one year. Should an appropriate position
open within that time, you will be contacted.

     Your interest in our company is appreciated. We wish you success in your job search.

                  Sincerely,

_____

Personnel Manager

NO DECISION ON HIRING

Date:

To:

Dear   :

    Thank you for your interest in employment with our company. You were among many well-qualified applicants who responded to our opening for a

                                                                               .

    Unfortunately, we have decided not to fill the position at this time.

    We will keep your resume on file for six months and will contact you should we decide to fill this position within that period.

    Thank you and good luck in your job search.

                                            Sincerely,

                                          _____

                                          Personnel Manager

EMPLOYMENT CONFIRMATION

Date:

To:

Dear   :

     I want to welcome you to our company as   .
This position is important to our organization and we look forward to having you
contribute your experience and expertise.

     Your first day of employment is   . Your salary will be
$ per   . After completing our 90- day evaluation period, you
will be eligible to participate in our medical, dental and life insurance benefits. Long-term
disability and family coverage under our medical plan is also available at your cost.

     While we want to start out on a positive note, it is important to understand that our
company is an "at will" employer. We think it is also important to understand that either
of us can terminate our employment arrangement at any time.

We are pleased to have you on board. Best wishes for success in your new position.

          Sincerely,

          _____
          Personnel Manager

Section 2

Employment Agreements

Form I201 **Independent Contractor's Agreement** – Contract for services from an independent contractor.

Form E201 **Employment Agreement** – Contract with employee outlining terms of employment.

Form A201 **Addendum to Employment Agreement** – Changes or adds provisions to an existing agreement.

Form A202 **Agreement with Sales Representative** – Contract with sales representative outlining terms of contract.

Form L201 **Letter Extending Sales Representative Agreement** – Extends length of contract by a specified time.

Form C201 **Change in Terms of Sales Representative Agreement** – Changes terms of an existing sales representative agreement.

Form C202 **Conflict of Interest Declaration** – Employee acknowledges company's prohibition of conflict of interest and affirms none between employee's personal affairs and responsibilities for the company.

Form C203 **Consent for Drug/Alcohol Screen Testing** – Gives employee's permission to be tested for drug and alcohol use.

Form P201 **Polygraph Examination Consent Form** – Gives employee's permission to undergo a lie detector test.

Form A203 **Agreement to Accept Night Work** – Makes night work a condition of employment with company.

Form E202 **Expense Recovery Agreement** – Employee agrees to repay company for any disallowed expense deductions for which employee was reimbursed.

Form A204 **Agreement on Inventions and Patents** – Employee agrees to non-disclosure of company information regarding inventions and patents.

Form A205	**Agreement on Proprietary Rights** – Releases company from any liability with regard to submission of suggestions, ideas or inventions from employee.
Form E203	**Employee's Agreement on Confidential Data** – Employee agrees to non-disclosure of confidential company information.
Form C204	**Confidentiality Agreement** – Employee agrees to keep information about company and employees confidential.
Form E204	**Employee's Covenants** – Employee agrees to be liable for any disclosure of trade secrets or solicitation or promotion of another company similar to employer.
Form E205	**Employee Secrecy Agreement** – Employee agrees to keep all knowledge and information gained from employment a secret.
Form G201	**General Non-Compete Agreement** – Employee agrees to not compete with employer for a specified period upon termination.
Form N201	**Non-Compete Agreement (Accounts)** – Employee agrees to not solicit employer's customers or accounts for a specified period upon termination.
Form N202	**Non-Compete Agreement (Area)** – Employee agrees to not engage in a similar business to employer in a specified geographic area for a specified period upon termination.
Form N203	**Non-Disclosure of Trade Secrets** – Employee agrees to non- disclosure of employer's trade secrets during and after termination of employment.
Form A206	**Acknowledgement of Temporary Employment** – Employee acknowledges rights as a temporary employee.
Form E206	**Employer Indemnity Agreement** – Releases company from liability due to wrongdoing or neglect on the part of employee.
Form E207	**Employee Indemnity** – Releases employee from liability as a result of any wrongdoing or neglect on the part of the company.
Form W201	**Waiver of Liability** – Releases company from any liability associated with employee's participation in company recreational activities.

INDEPENDENT CONTRACTOR'S AGREEMENT

Contract made on this   day of   , 19   ,
between: , herein referred to as Owner, doing
business at   , City of
                    State of   , and
                                   , herein referred to as Contractor, doing business
at   , City of
                    State of   .

RECITALS

1. Owner operates a   business
at the address set forth above and desires to have the following services performed at
Owner's place of business:

2. Contractor agrees to perform these services for Owner under the terms and
conditions set forth in this contract.

In consideration of the mutual promises contained herein, it is agreed:

A. Description of Work: The Contractor shall perform all services generally related
to Contractor's usual line of business, including, but not limited to, the following:

B. Payment: Owner will pay Contractor the sum of

Dollars ($) for the work

performed under this contract, under the following schedule:

C. Relationship of Parties: This contract creates an independent contractor-employer relationship. Owner is interested only in the results to be achieved. Contractor is solely responsible for the conduct and control of the work. Contractor is not an agent or employee of Owner for any purpose. Employees of Contractor are not entitled to any benefits that Owner provides Owner's employees. This is not an exclusive agreement. Both parties are free to contract with other parties for similar services.

D. Liability: Contractor assumes all risk connected with work to be performed. Contractor also accepts all responsibility for the condition of tools and equipment used in the performance of this contract and will carry for the duration of this contract public liability insurance in an amount acceptable to Owner. Contractor agrees to indemnify Owner for any and all liability or loss arising from the performance of this contract.

E. Duration: Either party may cancel this contract with   days' written notice; otherwise, the contract shall remain in force for a term of   from date hereof.

In witness whereof, the parties have executed this agreement in the City of

, State of   , the day and year first above written.

_____   _____
(Signature of Owner)   (Signature of Contractor)

EMPLOYMENT AGREEMENT

Agreement dated   , 19   , between
(hereinafter the Company) and
(hereinafter the Employee).

      The Company employs the Employee, and the Employee agrees to be employed, on the following terms and conditions:

      1. **Term of Employment.** Subject to the provisions for earlier termination herein, employment will begin on   , 19   .

      2. **Salary.** The Company shall pay Employee a salary of $ per year, payable:

      3. **Duties and Position.** The Company hires the Employee in the capacity as   , and Employee's duties will generally be:

The Employee's duties may be reasonably changed, increased or reduced at the Company's direction.

      4. **Employee to Serve as Officer If Elected.** Should the Employee be elected or appointed a director or officer of the Company during his employment, the Employee shall serve in such office without further compensation. The Company is not required by this agreement to cause the election or appointment of the Employee.

      5. **Employee Shall Devote Full Time to Company.** The Employee will devote full time and attention to the business of the Company, and, during his or her employment, will not engage in any other business activity, regardless of whether such activity is pursued for profit, gain, or other pecuniary advantage. However, the Employee is not prohibited from making personal investments in any other businesses, so long as those investments do not require Employee to participate in the operation of the companies in which he or she invests.

      6. **Confidentiality of Customer List.** Since the list of the Company's customers is a valuable, special, and unique asset of the Company, the Employee agrees, during or after the term of his employment, not to reveal the list, or any part of it, or other trade secret to any person, firm, corporation, association, or any other entity. The Company shall be entitled to restrain the Employee from disclosing the list, or any other trade secret, or from rendering any services to any entity to whom the list has been or is threatened to be disclosed. The right to an injunction is not exclusive, and the Company may pursue any other remedies it has against the Employee for a breach or threatened breach of this condition, including the recovery of damages.

7. **Expense Reimbursement.** The Employee may incur reasonable expenses, including expenses for entertainment, travel, and similar items. The Company shall reimburse the Employee for all business expenses after the Employee presents an itemized account of his expenditures.

8. **Vacation.** Employee is entitled to a yearly vacation of   weeks at full pay. The Employee shall take his yearly vacation over a consecutive period beginning on or after   and ending on or before   .

9. **Disability.** If the Employee cannot perform hereunder because of illness or incapacity for a period of more than   weeks, the compensation otherwise due Employee during said illness or incapacity shall be reduced by   percent. Employee's full compensation shall be reinstated upon return to work. However, if the Employee is continuously absent from work for any reason for a period of over   months, the Company may terminate Employee and the Company's obligations under this agreement shall be discharged on that date.

10. **Termination of Agreement.** Without cause, the Company may terminate this agreement at any time upon   days' written notice to the Employee. Should the Company request, the Employee shall continue to work and be paid up to the date of termination. In addition, the Company shall pay Employee upon termination a severance allowance of $, less deductions required to be withheld. Further, without cause, the Employee may terminate this agreement upon   days' written notice to the Company. Employee shall work and be paid the regular salary up to the date of termination, but will not receive a severance allowance. In addition, and notwithstanding anything to the contrary contained in this agreement, the Company may terminate the Employee's employment upon   days' notice to the Employee upon any of the following events:

   (a) Sale of substantially all of the Company's assets to a single purchaser or group of associated purchasers; or

   (b) Sale, exchange, or other disposition of   percent or more of the Company's outstanding corporate shares; or

   (c) Company's termination of its business, or

   (d) Merger or consolidation of the Company in a transaction in which the Company's shareholders receive less than   percent of the outstanding voting shares of the surviving corporation.

11. **Death Benefit.** The Company will pay to the Employee's estate, upon death, any compensation due Employee up to the end of the month in which the Employee dies.

12. **Non-Competition.** For   years after the end of this agreement, the Employee shall not, within a   -mile radius of the Company's present place of business, directly or indirectly own, manage, operate, or control any business similar to that presently conducted by the Company.

13. **Effect of Prior Agreement.** This agreement supersedes any prior agreement between the Company or any predecessor of the Company and the Employee, except that this agreement shall not affect or operate to reduce any benefit or compensation inuring to the Employee of a kind elsewhere provided and not expressly provided in this agreement.

14. **Settlement by Arbitration.** Any claim or controversy that arises out of or relates to this agreement, or the breach thereof, will be settled by arbitration in the office nearest the Company in accordance with the prevailing rules of the American Arbitration Association. Judgment upon the award rendered may be entered in any court possessing jurisdiction of arbitration awards.

15. **Limited Effect of Waiver by Company.** If the Company waives a breach of any provision of this agreement by the Employee, that waiver will not operate or be construed as a waiver of any succeeding breach by the Employee.

16. **Severability.** If, for any reason, any provision of this agreement is held invalid, the other provisions of this agreement will remain in effect, insofar as is consistent with law. If this agreement is held invalid or cannot be enforced, then to the full extent permitted by law any prior agreement between the Company (or any predecessor thereof) and the Employee will be deemed reinstated as if this agreement had not been executed.

17. **Assumption of Agreement by Successors and Assignees.** The rights and obligations under this agreement will inure to the benefit and be binding upon the parties and their successors and assignees.

18. **Oral Modifications Not Binding.** This instrument is the entire agreement. Oral changes will have no effect. This agreement may be altered only by a written agreement signed by the party against whom enforcement of any waiver, change, modification, extension, or discharge is sought.

In Witness whereof, the parties have executed this agreement on

, 19   .

_____
Company

_____
By

_____
Employee

FORM E201 *Continued*

ADDENDUM TO EMPLOYMENT AGREEMENT

Reference is made to a certain agreement by and between
_____ (Employee) and
_____ (Company), said agreement being dated _____ , 19 _____ .

BE IT KNOWN, that for good consideration Employee and Company make the following additions or changes a part of said agreement as if contained therein:

All other terms and provisions of said agreement shall remain in full force and effect.

Signed this _____ day of _____ , 19 _____ .

_____
Company

_____
By

_____
Employee

AGREEMENT WITH SALES REPRESENTATIVE

Agreement dated   , 19   , between
(the Company) and
(the Sales Representative).

THE SALES REPRESENTATIVE AGREES TO:

1. Represent and sell the Company's line described as:

within the geographic area of:

2. State accurately company policies to all potential customers.

3. Promptly submit all orders to the sales manager.

4. Notify the sales manager of all problems of concern to the Company relating to customers within the sales territory.

5. Inform the sales manager if the Sales Representative is representing, or plans to represent, any other business firm. In no event may the Sales Representative represent a competitive product line.

6. Telephone the sales manager at least   to discuss sales activity in the territory.

7. Give one month's notice in writing to the sales manager if the Sales Representative wishes to terminate this agreement.

8. Promptly return all materials provided by the Company to the Sales Representative, if either party terminates this agreement.

THE COMPANY AGREES:

1. To pay the following commissions to the Sales Representative:

2. To negotiate in advance of sale the commission percentage to be paid on all orders where the Sales Representative requests a quantity discount or other trade concession be granted to a customer.

3. Refunds to customers or merchandise returned by the customer where a commission has already been paid to the Sales Representative, shall be deducted from future commissions to be paid to the Sales Representative.

4. For purposes of sales credit, a sale is defined as an order from a customer that was initiated by the personal action of the Sales Representative and delivered by the Sales Representative to the sales department of the Company.

5. Company shall provide the Sales Representative with business cards, brochures, catalogs, and any product samples required for demonstration purposes.

6. Company shall set minimum monthly quotas after consultation with the Sales Representative.

7. Company shall give one month's notice, in writing, if the Company wishes to terminate this agreement.

8. To pay all commissions owed to the Sales Representative for a period of months after this agreement is terminated by either party. Nothing in this agreement grants an exclusive sales territory to the Sales Representative. The Company shall continue to send direct mail advertising and have telemarketers solicit within the assigned territory of the Sales Representative.

_____   _____
Company   Sales Representative

_____
By

_____   _____
Date   Date

LETTER EXTENDING SALES REPRESENTATIVE AGREEMENT

Date:

To:

     This letter confirms the extension of our agreement made by and between
(Sales Representative), and
(Company), said Agreement being dated
, 19   .

     Whereas said Agreement expires on   , 19   ,
and the parties desire to extend and continue said Agreement; it is provided that said
Agreement shall be extended for an additional term commencing upon the expiration of
the original term with the new term expiring on   , 19   .

     This extension shall be on the same terms and conditions as contained in the original
Agreement and as if set forth and incorporated herein excepting only for the following
modification to the original Agreement:

     This extension of Agreement shall be binding upon and inure to the benefit of the
parties, their successors and assigns.

_____
Company

_____
By

Acknowledged:

_____
Sales Representative

_____
Date

CHANGE IN TERMS
OF SALES REPRESENTATIVE AGREEMENT

Date:

To:

    Reference is made to the contract between us dated   ,
19   , a copy of which is attached.

    This letter will acknowledge that the contract is modified and superseded by the following agreed change in terms:

    All other terms shall remain as stated.

    Unless we immediately hear from you to the contrary, in writing, we shall accept said modification as mutually agreeable, and shall proceed on the modified terms.

Very truly,

_____

Company

_____

By

The foregoing modification is acknowledged:

_____

Sales Representative

CONFLICT OF INTEREST DECLARATION

Employee:

Company:

    I acknowledge that I have read the Company policy statement concerning conflicts of interest and I hereby declare that neither I, nor any other business to which I may be associated, nor, to the best of my knowledge, any member of my immediate family has any conflict between our personal affairs or interests and the proper performance of my responsibilities for the Company that would constitute a violation of that Company policy. Furthermore, I declare that during my employment, I shall continue to maintain my affairs in accordance with the requirements of said policy.

_____

Employee's Signature

_____

Date

FORM C202

CONSENT FOR DRUG/ALCOHOL SCREEN TESTING

I ,   , have been fully informed by my potential employer of the reasons for this urine test for drug and/or alcohol. I understand what I am being tested for, the procedure involved, and do hereby freely give my consent. In addition, I understand that the results of this test will be forwarded to my potential employer and become part of my record.

If this test result is positive and for this reason I am not hired, I understand that I will be given the opportunity to explain the results of this test.

I hereby authorize these test results to be released to:

_____   _____
Signature   Date

_____   _____
Witness   Date

POLYGRAPH EXAMINATION CONSENT FORM

Name:_____ Social Security No.:_____
　　　　　(Please Print)

Date of Polygraph Examination:_____

I voluntarily agree to a polygraph examination on the above date.

A company representative has advised me of the following:

1. I am guaranteed by law the right not to take this examination as a condition of employment or continued employment.

2. I have not been coerced or forced in any way into either taking this test or signing this consent agreement.

3. I can retain a copy of this agreement for my records.

_____　　　_____
Signature　　　　　　　　　　　　　　　　Date

_____　　　_____
Witness　　　　　　　　　　　　　　　　　Date

AGREEMENT TO ACCEPT NIGHT WORK

A second shift is or may be required to meet our present or future needs. All new employees are hired with the understanding that they are able and willing to work nights.

Please answer the following:

	YES	NO
1. Do you have any physical disability that would prevent you from working nights?	_____	_____
2. Do you know of any personal reasons that would interfere with your working nights?	_____	_____
3. Are you willing to work nights?	_____	_____

I understand that any employment is conditioned upon my acceptance of a night assignment if required. Furthermore, I understand that I can be reassigned by the company to any plant or department. However, my requests for transfer will be considered only after I have successfully completed the requisite period of active employment with the company.

_____
Signed

_____
Date

_____
Witness

In case of emergency notify:

Name:_____ Phone: _____

Address:_____ Relationship: _____

Name:_____ Phone: _____

Address:_____ Relationship: _____

EXPENSE RECOVERY AGREEMENT

The undersigned Employee of _____ (Employer) hereby agrees to repay to Employer all amounts paid by the Employer to the Employee as compensation for or reimbursement of expenses incurred in the course of employment that are disallowed, in whole or in part, as deductible to the Employer for income tax purposes.

In the presence of:

_____   _____
Employee   Date

_____   _____
Witness   Date

FORM E202

AGREEMENT ON INVENTIONS
AND PATENTS

Agreement made between
(Company) and   (Employee)
this   day of   , 19   .

In consideration of the employment or continued employment of Employee by Company, the parties agree to the following:

1. Employee may have access to apparatus, equipment, drawings, reports, manuals, inventions, customer lists, computer programs, or other trade secrets or confidential, technical or business information of Company or its affiliates. Employee therein agrees

    (a)   not to use any such trade secrets, inventions, information or material hereto for himself or others, and

    (b)   not to remove any such items or reproductions from Company facilities, either during or after employment by Company, except as absolutely required in Employee's duties to Company. Employee further agrees to immediately return all such items and reproductions thereof in his possession to Company upon request, and in any event upon termination of employment.

2. Employee agrees not to disclose or publish any trade secret or confidential technical or business information of Company or its affiliates or of another party to whom Company owes an obligation of confidentiality, either during or after employment by Company, unless Employee has prior written authorization by the Company.

3. Employee shall promptly provide Company a complete record of any and all inventions and improvements, whether patentable or not, which Employee, solely or jointly, may conceive, make, or first disclose during the said employment.

4. Employee hereby grants, assigns and delivers to Company, or its nominee, Employee's entire right, title, and interest in and to all inventions and improvements coming within the scope of Paragraph 3 that relate in any way to the actual or anticipated business or activities of Company, or its affiliates, or that are suggested by or result from any task or work for or on behalf of Company or its affiliates, together with any and all domestic and foreign patent rights in such inventions and improvements. To assist Company or its nominee in securing patents thereto, Employee agrees promptly to do all lawful and reasonable things both during and after employment, without additional compensation, but at Company's expense.

5. Employee agrees that, upon accepting employment with any organization in competition with Company or its affiliates during a period of   year(s) following employment termination, Employee shall notify Company in writing within thirty days of the name and address of such new employer.

6. Employee agrees to give Company timely written notice of any prior employment agreements or patent rights that may conflict with the interests of Company or its affiliates.

7. No waiver by either party of any breach by the other party of any provision of this agreement shall be deemed or construed to be a waiver of a later breach of such provision.

8. This agreement shall be binding upon and inure to the benefit of the parties and their successors and assigns.

9. Where inconsistent, this agreement supersedes the terms of any prior employment agreement or understanding between Employee and Company. This Agreement may be modified or amended only in writing, duly signed by Company and Employee.

10. It is agreed that this agreement will be interpreted and construed according to the laws of the state where Company is located. Should any portion of this agreement be judicially held to be invalid, unenforceable or void, then such holding shall not invalidate the remainder of this agreement or any other part thereof.

_____
Date

_____   _____
Company Name   Employee's Full Name

Employee acknowledges reading, understanding and receiving a signed copy of this agreement.

_____   _____
By (Company Officer)   Date

_____   _____
Employee's Signature   Date

FORM A204 *Continued*

AGREEMENT ON PROPRIETARY RIGHTS

Date:

Idea for:

     I represent to   (Company) that I now have suggestions, ideas or inventions, and may, in the future, have related suggestions, which I now request the Company to consider for commercial exploitation. I understand that the Company cannot accept such suggestions in confidence; therefore, I agree to submit my suggestions to the Company under the following conditions:

     1. The Company's review of my suggestions is made only upon my request, and the Company accepts no responsibility for holding any submitted information in confidence.

     2. No obligation of any kind is assumed nor may be implied against the Company unless or until I have entered into a formal written contract with the Company pertaining to my submissions. In addition, any obligation shall be only such as is expressed in writing.

     3. Neither the Company nor any of its affiliates shall have any rights under any patents I now have nor may later obtain for my submissions covered by this letter, but, in consideration of their examining and considering same, I hereby release the Company from any liability in connection with my submissions or from liability because of their use of my submissions or of any portion thereof, except such liability as may accrue under valid patents now or hereafter issued. Subject to these conditions, I certify that I have made no prior disclosure to the Company or any of its affiliates regarding these submissions and that the entire disclosure now made by me to the Company is included in the attached papers listed below and submitted for retention by the Company. If, at any time, I correspond with or discuss my submissions with an officer, employee, agent or representative of the Company and, in the course of such correspondence or discussion, make any additional disclosures regarding such submissions, I shall, upon request, furnish the Company an illustration or a complete description, or both, of such additional disclosure, so that it can be made a part of the permanent record of the Company.

_____

Date

_____

Submitted by

_____

Address of Submitter

The following documents are attached and made a part of this agreement.

1. _____

2. _____

3. _____

4. _____

5. _____

6. _____

7. _____

8. _____

9. _____

10. _____

FORM A205 *Continued*

EMPLOYEE'S AGREEMENT ON CONFIDENTIAL DATA

I, the undersigned,   , acknowledge
that I have received all salary, earnings and other compensation due me during my
employment by the Company, which terminated on   ,
19   . I certify that I have not done, or in any way been a party to, or knowingly
permitted:

  1. Disclosure of any confidential matters or trade secrets of the Company.

  2. Retention or copying of any confidential materials or documents issued to or used
by me or others during my employment.

  I acknowledge that I have again been carefully and fully advised by the Company of
my continuing obligations to preserve as confidential, and not to reveal to anyone or use,
for myself or anyone else, any trade secrets or confidential matters learned by me during,
or by reason of, my employment by the Company and I reaffirm such obligations. I agree
that the Company may inform, in writing, my new employer, of my said obligations,
provided only that I receive a copy of such letter or other related communication.

_____   _____
Employee   Date

CONFIDENTIALITY AGREEMENT

The nature of services provided by
(Company) requires information to be handled in a private, confidential manner.

Information about our business or our employees or clients will only be released to people or agencies outside the company with our written consent. Following legal or regulatory guidelines provide the only exceptions to this policy. All reports, memoranda, notes, or other documents will remain part of the company's confidential records.

The names, addresses, phone numbers or salaries of our employees will only be released to people authorized by the nature of their duties to receive such information and only with the consent of management or the employee.

The undersigned employee agrees to abide by this confidentiality agreement.

_____   _____
Employee   Date

_____   _____
Witness   Date

FORM C204

EMPLOYEE'S COVENANTS

                                    (Employee), a resident of
           and employed by or about to be
employed by   (Company),
hereby makes these covenants to Company in consideration for

_____hiring Employee in the position of
_____continued employment of Employee, with the following change in the nature of employment:

COVENANT 1

Employee's Covenants

During the term of employment and one (1) year after termination, Employee agrees to refrain from the following:

1. Promoting or engaging in indirectly or directly, as an employee, principal, partner, contractor, associate, agent, manager or otherwise, or by means of any entity, any business in the same or similar business as Company or its affiliates within the following geographic area:

2. Soliciting Company's customers, employees, staff, vendors, subcontractors, or prospects with services or products of the nature of those being sold by Company or affiliates of Company.

3. Employee agrees Company and its affiliates hold certain trade, business, and financial secrets in connection with the business. Employee covenants to not divulge to any party at any time, directly or indirectly, during the term of this Agreement or afterwards, unless directed by the Board of Directors, any information acquired by Employee about Company or its affiliates, including, but not limited to, customer lists, trade secrets, documents, financial statements, quotes, correspondence, patents, processes, formulas, research, intellectual property, expenses, costs or other confidential information of any kind, or any other data that could be used by third parties to the disadvantage of Company. This paragraph shall survive the term of employment.

COVENANT 2

Company Rights on Breach

If Employee breaches this covenant, Company shall have the right, in addition to all other rights available hereunder and by law, to enjoin Employee from continuing such breach. Employee affirms having the opportunity to fully discuss and negotiate this Covenant and acknowledges understanding and acceptance. If any part of this Covenant is declared invalid, then Employee agrees to be bound by a Covenant as near to the original as lawfully possible. This paragraph shall survive the term and termination of employment. Employee shall further be liable for all costs of enforcement.

COVENANT 3

Additional Governing Terms

No waiver of a right by Company constitutes a waiver of any other right of Company, and temporary waiver by Company does not constitute a permanent waiver or any additional temporary waiver. These Covenants may be modified only in writing and signed by Employee and Company. If any portion of these Covenants is declared invalid, these Covenants shall continue in effect as if the invalid portion had never been part hereof. Covenants shall be governed under the laws of the State of

_____   _____
Employee   Date

_____
Company

_____   _____
By   Date

EMPLOYEE SECRECY AGREEMENT

I,   , as an employee of
                                    (Company), acknowledge
that I have access to such trade secrets as

                                                              .

All knowledge and information I gain from those trade secrets and the trade secrets themselves, including all unpatented inventions, designs, know-how, trade secrets, technical information and data, specifications, blueprints, transparencies, test data, and additions, modifications, and improvements thereon which are revealed to me shall for all time be regarded by me as strictly confidential. I will only reveal or disclose the trade secrets to another person, firm, corporation, company or entity if my employer instructs me to do so in writing. This secrecy protection will continue even after my dismissal by
                                    . I acknowledge that if I reveal the trade secrets to unauthorized persons I may be penalized and sued for injunctive relief and money damages as well as face possible criminal charges by my employer.

I have read and understand the contents of this Agreement and voluntarily sign it with the intent to be legally bound hereby.

_____   _____
Employee   Date

_____   _____
Witness   Date

GENERAL NON-COMPETE AGREEMENT

For good consideration and as an inducement for

(Company) to employ   (Employee),
the undersigned Employee hereby agrees not to directly or indirectly compete with the business of the Company during the period of employment and for a period of   years thereafter following termination of employment and notwithstanding the cause or reason for termination.

The term "not compete" shall mean that the Employee shall not directly or indirectly own, operate, consult to or be employed by any firm in a business substantially similar to or competitive with the present business of the Company or such business activity in which the Company may engage during the term of employment.

The Employee hereby acknowledges that the Company shall or may in reliance of this agreement provide Employee access to trade secrets, customers and other confidential data, and that this agreement is reasonably necessary to protect the Company.

This agreement shall be binding upon and inure to the benefit of the parties, their heirs, assigns and personal representatives.

Signed under seal this   day of   , 19   .

_____
Company

_____
By

_____
Employee

FORM G201

NON-COMPETE AGREEMENT (ACCOUNTS)

For valuable consideration and as an inducement for

(Company)

to employ
(Employee),

the undersigned Employee agrees not to directly or indirectly compete with the Company during the period of employment and for a period of   years thereafter and notwithstanding the cause or reason for termination.

The term "not compete" shall mean that the Employee shall not, on Employee's behalf or on behalf of any other party, solicit or seek the business of any customer or account of the Company existing during the term of employment and wherein said solicitation involves a product and/or service substantially similar to or competitive with any present or future product and/or service of the Company.

The Employee hereby acknowledges that the Company shall or may provide Employee access to its customers and accounts in reliance of this agreement, and that this agreement is reasonably necessary to protect the Company.

This agreement shall be binding upon and inure to the benefit of the parties, their heirs, assigns and personal representatives.

Signed under seal this   day of   , 19   .

_____
Company

_____
By

_____
Employee

NON-COMPETE AGREEMENT (AREA)

For valuable consideration and as an inducement for

(Company)

to employ   (Employee),
the undersigned hereby agrees not to directly or indirectly compete with the business of
the Company during the period of employment or for a period of   years thereafter
and notwithstanding the cause or reason for termination.

The term "not compete" as used herein shall mean that the Employee shall not
directly or indirectly own, operate, consult to or be employed by any Company or entity
engaged in a business substantially similar to or competitive with any service and/or
product of the Company as now existing or as the Company may undertake during the
term of employment.

This covenant shall apply only to a radius of   (   ) miles from the
present location of the Company as set forth below, and to no prospects or customers
beyond said area.

The Employee acknowledges that the Company shall or may provide Employee
access to customers and trade secrets and other confidential or propriety information in
reliance of this agreement and that the provisions of this agreement are reasonably
necessary to protect the Company.

This agreement shall be binding upon and inure to the benefit of the parties, their
heirs, assigns and personal representatives.

Signed under seal this   day of   , 19   .

_____   _____
Employee   Company

                                        _____
                                        By

                                        _____
                                        Address

                                        _____

FORM N202

NON-DISCLOSURE OF TRADE SECRETS

In consideration of my being employed by
_____ (Company), the undersigned hereby agrees and acknowledges the following:

1.   That during my employment there may be disclosed to me certain trade secrets consisting of:

a)   Technical information: Methods, processes, formulae, compositions, systems, techniques, inventions, machines, computer programs and research projects.

b)   Business information: Customer lists, pricing data, sources of supply, and marketing, production, or merchandising systems or plans.

2.   I agree that during and after the termination of my employment, I shall not use for myself or others, or disclose or divulge to others any trade secrets, confidential information, or any other data of the Company in violation of this agreement.

3.   Upon terminating my employment with the Company:

a)   I shall return to the Company all documents and property pertaining to the Company, including but not limited to: drawings, blueprints, records, reports, manuals, correspondence, customer lists, computer programs, inventions, and all other materials and all copies thereof relating in any way to the Company's business, or in any way obtained by me during my employment. I further agree that I shall not retain any copies or reproductions of the foregoing.

b)   The Company may notify any future or prospective employer of this agreement.

c)   This agreement shall be binding upon me and my personal representatives and successors in interest, and shall inure to the benefit of the Company, its successors and assigns.

d)   The enforceability of any one provision to this agreement shall not impair or affect any other terms of this agreement.

e)   In the event of any breach of this agreement, the Company shall have full rights to injunctive relief, in addition to any other existing rights, without requirement of posting bond, if permitted by law.

_____   _____
Employee   Date

_____
Company

_____   _____
By   Date

ACKNOWLEDGEMENT OF TEMPORARY EMPLOYMENT

I, the undersigned, understand I am being employed by _____ (Company) in a temporary position only and for such time as my services are required. I hereby acknowledge that this temporary employment does not entitle me to any special consideration for permanent employment. I further understand that my temporary employment may be terminated at any time without resort to the handbook disciplinary procedures set forth for permanent employees. Furthermore, I understand that I am not eligible to participate in any fringe benefit programs or retirement program or any other programs available to permanent employees (unless required by law) and in the event I am allowed to participate in said benefit or program, then my continued participation may be voluntarily withdrawn or terminated by the Company at any time and without reason.

_____
Employee

_____
Date

_____
Witness

FORM A206

EMPLOYER INDEMNITY AGREEMENT

The undersigned, in consideration of being employed by _____ (Company) agrees to fully indemnify and save harmless the Company from any claim by any third party alleging wrongdoing or neglect on my part, and for any expense or loss incurred by the Company as a result of any violation of state or federal law, agency rule or regulation that was within the scope of my employment to obey or cause the Company to obey. Any claims for which the Company is adequately insured and/or any liability to which the Company or any other employee shares responsibility are exempt from this indemnity.

In the event of any asserted claim against the company, I will defend at my own expense, save harmless, indemnify and reimburse the Company for any loss or liability that may arise from such asserted claim.

_____
Date:

_____
Print Name

_____
Company

_____
Employee's Signature

_____
By

EMPLOYEE INDEMNITY

In consideration and as an inducement of
_____ (Employee) being employed by the
Company as a _____ and in
recognition of the company's reliance on Employee's skill and experience; Company agrees to fully indemnify and save harmless Employee from any claim by any third party alleging neglect or wrongdoing on Employee's part, or loss or expense as a result of any violation of law that was within the scope of Employee's employment to obey. Exempted from this indemnity agreement shall be such claims against which the Company is adequately insured and/or any liability to which the Company or any other employee shares responsibility.

In the event of any asserted claim against Employee and upon reasonable notice of such claim, then Company shall at its own expense defend, indemnify, save harmless and reimburse the Employee for any loss or liability that may arise from such claim.

This indemnity agreement shall be binding upon and inure to the benefit of the parties, their successors, assigns and personal representatives.

Signed under seal this _____ day of _____ , 19 _____ .

_____
Company

_____
By

Acknowledged:

_____
Employee

_____
Date

WAIVER OF LIABILITY

I,   (Employee),
hereby release   (Company)
from any and all liability connected with my participation in company recreational
activities. I acknowledge that I am participating in these activities on my own time and of
my own choice and assume all risk in connection thereto.

_____

Employee

_____

Date

_____

Witness

Section 3
Processing New Employees

Form R301   **Rehire Form** – Records pertinent information on previous employees.

Form H301   **Hiring Authorization** – Authorizes hiring of personnel.

Form R302   **Relocation Expense Approval** – Authorizes payment of new employee's relocation expenses.

Form L301   **Letter to New Employee 1** – Informs a new employee of the date to report to work.

Form L302   **Letter to New Employee 2** – Welcomes a new employee.

Form L303   **Letter to New Employee 3** – Informs a new employee of the date and time to report to work.

Form L304   **Letter to New Employee 4** – Welcomes a new employee and informs him/her of the date and time to report to work.

Form N301   **New Employee Announcement** – Announces the addition of a new employee.

Form E301   **Employee Background Verification** – Verifies the background of an employee.

Form N302   **New Employee Orientation Checklist** – Lists information to be reviewed with new employees.

Form N303   **New Employee Checklist** – Lists information on employee to be in file before beginning work.

Form N304   **New Personnel Checklist** – Lists information to be obtained from new employee.

Form E302   **Employee Agreement and Handbook Acknowledgement** – Acknowledges employee's receipt of Employee Agreement and Handbook.

Form J301	**Job Description** – Describes an employee's position, function, authority level and scope of work.
Form E303	**Emergency Procedures** – Describes steps to take in a particular emergency.
Form S301	**Summary of Employment Terms** – Summarizes terms of employment.
Form P301	**Payroll Deduction Authorization** – Authorizes specific deductions from an employee's paycheck.
Form P302	**Payroll Deduction Direct Deposit Authorization** – Authorizes direct deposit of a specific payroll deduction.
Form D301	**Direct Deposit Authorization** - Authorizes direct deposit of an employee's paycheck.
Form W301	**Withholding Tax Information** – Records an employee's withholding tax information.
Form E304	**Employee File** – Records an employee's history with the company.
Form N305	**New Employee Data** – Records information about a new employee.
Form E305	**Emergency Phone Numbers** – Records emergency phone number information from a new employee.
Form E306	**Employee Health Evaluation (Pre-Employment)** – Obtains detailed information regarding an employee's health.
Form C301	**Consent for Drug/Alcohol Screening** – Consents to drug or alcohol testing as a condition of employment.
Form R303	**Receipt for Company Property** – Records company property issued to employee.
Form S302	**Samples and Documents Receipt** – Records samples and documents issued to employee.
Form E307	**EEO Analysis of New Hires** – Analyzes the minority makeup of new hires.

REHIRE FORM

To help us keep our files current, please complete the following:

Personal Information:

Name:_____ Home Phone: _____

Address: _____

Social Security Number: _____ Work Phone:_____

Current employer:_____

Previous Employment Information:

Original Hire Date: _____

Department:_____ Return Date: _____

Position: _____ Position Number:_____

Salary: _____ Review Date:_____

Emergency Information:

Name:_____ Phone: _____

Address_____

Relationship _____

To my best knowledge the above information is correct.

_____   _____
Signature   Date

FORM R301

HIRING AUTHORIZATION

Date: _____

Applicant: _____

Title/Job: _____

_____

_____

P/T ( )   F/T ( )   Permanent ( )   Temporary ( )

Starting Salary: $ _____ Starting Date: _____

Supervisor: _____

Replacement ( )   New Position ( )

Department: _____ Budget: _____

Description of Duties: _____

_____

_____

_____

_____

Approval to Hire is   _____ granted

                             _____ not granted

Comments: _____

_____

_____

_____

_____

_____ By: _____

RELOCATION EXPENSE APPROVAL

Employee: _____ Social Security No.:_____

Account to be Charged: _____ Position: _____

Prior Location: _____ New Location: _____

Effective Date of Hire: _____ Present Residence: Own _____ Rent _____

Married _____ Single _____ Head of Household _____ # of Dependents _____

	Estimated Cost	Actual Cost
1. Cost of moving household goods	$_____	$_____
2. Employee travel and lodging to new location	$_____	$_____
3. Family travel and lodging to new location	$_____	$_____
4. Househunting travel and lodging for employee up to 4 days	$_____	$_____
5. Incidental expense allowance of 3/4 of 1 month's salary	$_____	$_____
6. Federal income tax allowance	$_____	$_____
7. Other special items (specify)	$_____	$_____
_____	$_____	$_____
_____	$_____	$_____
_____	$_____	$_____

Employee's Signature_____ Date_____

Approvals:

Department Manager:_____ Date_____

President:_____ Date_____
(If required)

FORM R302

Date:

To:

Dear   :

    This acknowledges your acceptance of our employment offer. We are pleased you have decided to join our company and look forward to your reporting on

    .

    As discussed, we will pay your moving and travel expenses according to company policy. We will make the necessary arrangement to move your furniture with a transportation company. Please submit your personal transportation expenses to us at the time you report for work.

    Again, we are happy you have made the decision to accept our offer. Please do not hesitate to let us know if we can assist you in any way.

                          Very truly yours,

                          _____

Date:

To:

Dear   :

It is a pleasure to welcome you as a new member of

                                                                        . You are now

part of   .

As you become more familiar with your duties and better acquainted with the other members of our company, you will find that all of us have an important part to play.

My warmest wishes to you on beginning your employment with us.

Very truly yours,

_____

Date:

To:

Dear   :

    At   m. ,   19   , you are to report for work at
the personnel office of   .
We hope you are looking forward to this event as enthusiastically as we are.

    You are now a member of a fine group of people operating as a team with the
common objective of providing

                                                                            .

    We are very happy that you have chosen us for your career. We look forward to
seeing you on your starting day.

                                               Very truly yours,

                                    _____

Date:

To:

Dear   :

        Your career with our company will begin on   , 19   , at
m. We welcome you with great pleasure.

        We are both now being offered an opportunity to establish and develop a mutually
rewarding relationship. It is with a great deal of confidence that we look forward to
achieving this goal.

        So again, welcome. If you have any questions, please let us know.

                                                        Very truly yours,

                                                        _____

NEW EMPLOYEE ANNOUNCEMENT

Date:

To: All Employees

From:

Subject: New Employee

     I am pleased to announce that   has
joined our staff as   . In this new
position,   will report to   .

     Our new employee comes to us from   ,
where
and prior to that was   .

     Please join me in welcoming   to our
company and in wishing   much success!

_____
Signed

EMPLOYEE BACKGROUND VERIFICATION

Applicant Name: _____ Date: _____

Position Applied for: _____

Date of Application: _____

	Requested	Received	Comments
Education/Schools:			
_____	_____	_____	_____
_____	_____	_____	_____
_____	_____	_____	_____
Prior Employment:			
_____	_____	_____	_____
_____	_____	_____	_____
_____	_____	_____	_____
Military Service:			
_____	_____	_____	_____
_____	_____	_____	_____
_____	_____	_____	_____
Other:			
_____	_____	_____	_____
_____	_____	_____	_____
_____	_____	_____	_____

Completed by : _____

FORM E301

NEW EMPLOYEE ORIENTATION CHECKLIST

Employee: _____ Position: _____

Starting Date: _____ Interview Date: _____

Supervisor: _____

	To Be Reviewed (Check)	Reviewed (Check)
Conditions of Employment	_____	_____
Probationary Period	_____	_____
Union Memberships	_____	_____
Work Schedule	_____	_____
Vacations/Holidays	_____	_____
Attendance & Absences	_____	_____
Payroll Procedures	_____	_____
Credit Union	_____	_____
Parking	_____	_____
Lunch Break Schedule	_____	_____
Cafeteria Facilities	_____	_____
First Aid Facilities & Safety	_____	_____
Advancement Opportunities	_____	_____
Group Insurance	_____	_____
Life Insurance	_____	_____
Grievance Procedures	_____	_____
Day Care	_____	_____
Cafeteria Plans	_____	_____
General Fringe Benefits	_____	_____
Health Insurance	_____	_____
Pension/Retirement	_____	_____

Tuition Reimbursement   _____   _____

Changes in Personnel Records   _____   _____

Employee Policy Information   _____   _____

Employee Received:

Union Contract   _____

Union Information   _____

Safety Rules   _____

Group Insurance Information   _____

Life Insurance Information   _____

Medical Insurance Information   _____

Employee Policy   _____

Other: _____

_____   _____

_____   _____

_____   _____

_____
Personnel Representative

_____
Date

I acknowledge that the above checked items have been discussed to my satisfaction, and I also acknowledge receipt of the items checked.

_____
Employee

_____
Date

FORM N302 *Continued*

NEW EMPLOYEE CHECKLIST

Employee: _____   Position: _____

Department: _____   Starting Date: _____

New employees must have checked item(s) in file before beginning work.

Document	Required	Completed
Employment Application	_____	_____
Personal Data Sheet	_____	_____
Employee Verification Sheet	_____	_____
Polygraph Consent	_____	_____
Drug Testing Consent	_____	_____
Fidelity Bond	_____	_____
Physical/Medical Report	_____	_____
Employment Contract	_____	_____
Non-Competition Agreement	_____	_____
Confidentiality Agreement	_____	_____
Conflict of Interest Declaration	_____	_____
Indemnity Agreement	_____	_____
Security Clearance	_____	_____
Other:		
_____	_____	_____
_____	_____	_____
_____	_____	_____

_____
Supervisor

_____
Date

NEW PERSONNEL CHECKLIST

_____ Employment application

_____ Reference reports

_____ Formal job offer letter and employee acknowledgement

_____ Employment contract, confidentiality agreement

_____ Social Security Number

_____ Verification of citizenship or legal employment status, including Form I-9

_____ Federal, state, local tax withholding forms

_____ Insurance forms: health, group life, disability

_____ Physical examination reports

_____ Security records, bonding and fingerprint card

_____ Performance evaluations

_____ Retirement plan application

_____ Receipt for benefit plan options and elections

_____ Termination agreement and exit interview

FORM N304

EMPLOYEE AGREEMENT
AND HANDBOOK ACKNOWLEDGEMENT

This employee handbook and the personnel policy manual highlight the company policies, procedures, and benefits. In all instances the official benefit plan texts, trust agreements and master contracts are the governing documents. Your employee handbook is not to be interpreted as a legal document or an employment contract. Employment with the company is at the sole discretion of the company and may be terminated with or without cause at any time and for any reason. Nothing in this handbook or in the personnel policy manual constitutes an express or implied contract or assurance of continued employment, or implies that just cause is required for termination.

Understood and agreed:

_____
Employee

_____
Date

JOB DESCRIPTION

Position:

Basic Function:

Scope of work:

Principal Accountabilities:

Principal Interactions:

 Knowledge/Education Requirements:

Authority Level:

Reports to:

FORM J301

EMERGENCY PROCEDURES

The company's emergency procedures in case of crisis are as follows:

Fire:

Bomb Threat:

Tornado:

Hurricane:

Earthquake:

Snowstorm:

Dangerous or threatening person entering the building:

Media Crisis:

Other:

SUMMARY OF EMPLOYMENT TERMS

Date:

To:

    We are very pleased you have accepted a position with our company, and we want to take this opportunity to summarize your initial terms and conditions of employment.

1.   Commencement date of employment: _____

2.   Position/title: _____

3.   Starting salary: _____

4.   Weeks vacation/year: _____

5.   Eligible for vacation starting: _____

6.   Health insurance: _____

    _____

7.   Pension/Profit-Sharing: _____

    _____

8.   Other benefits: _____

    _____

9.   Other terms/conditions: _____

    _____

    If this does not accurately summarize your understanding, please notify me immediately. You understand, of course, that your employment may be terminated by either party at will, and we reserve the right to modify benefits, terms of employment, and employee policies.

    Again, we look forward to your joining us.

                             Very truly,

                             _____

PAYROLL DEDUCTION AUTHORIZATION

   The undersigned hereby authorizes _____ to deduct
$ _____ from my earnings each payroll period, beginning _____ ,
for the following:

In payment for: Amount

_____   Employee Savings Plan   _____

_____   Credit Union   _____

_____   401K Plan   _____

_____   Union Dues   _____

_____   _____   _____

_____   _____   _____

_____   _____   _____

_____   _____   _____

                                     Total $ _____

_____   _____
Signature   Date

Print Name: _____

Social Security No.: _____

Please retain a copy of this for your records.

PAYROLL DEDUCTION DIRECT DEPOSIT AUTHORIZATION

Name: _____

Identification No.: _____ Social Security No.:_____

Bank Name & Branch: _____

Account No.: _____

Check appropriate box:

[   ] Direct payroll deduction

The undersigned hereby requests and authorizes the sum of _____ dollars ($_____) be deducted from my paycheck each pay period and to be deposited directly into the bank account named above.

[   ] Cancellation of deposit authorization:

The undersigned hereby cancels the authorization for direct deposit previously submitted.

_____
Employee

_____
Date

Please attach copy of deposit slip.

FORM P302

DIRECT DEPOSIT AUTHORIZATION

Employee: _____

Identification No.: _____ Social Security No.: _____

Bank Name and Branch: _____

Account No.: _____

[   ] I hereby request the deposit of my entire net payroll check into the above-named bank account each pay period. I authorize and   to withdraw any funds deposited in error into my account.

[   ] I hereby request and authorize the sum of   dollars ($) to be deducted from my paycheck each pay period and to be deposited directly into the bank account named above.

[   ] I hereby cancel the authorization for direct deposit or payroll deduction deposit previously submitted.

_____
Employee

_____
Date

Please attach a copy of deposit slip.

WITHHOLDING TAX INFORMATION

Employee:_____

Address: _____

Position:_____ Supervisor: _____

Date Hired: _____ Payroll Date: _____

Social Security No.: _____ Spouse Social Security No.:_____

No. Dependents:_____ No. Exemptions: _____

Exemptions From State/Municipal Taxes (Attach Certificates of Exemption):

    The number of dependents claimed is accurate and I shall notify the personnel department of any change in dependents.

_____
Employee

_____
Date

Change in Number of Dependents

		Employee Initials	Date
From _____ dependents to_____ dependents		_____	_____
From _____ dependents to_____ dependents		_____	_____
From _____ dependents to_____ dependents		_____	_____
From _____ dependents to_____ dependents		_____	_____

EMPLOYEE FILE

Employee: _____

Address: _____

Phone: _____ Social Security No.:_____ DOB: _____

Sex: _____ M _____ F

Marital Status:

_____ Single _____ Married _____ Separated _____ Widowed _____ Divorced

Name of Spouse: _____ No. Dependents: _____

In Emergency Notify: _____ Relationship: _____

Address: _____

Education (No. Years): _____High School _____ College _____ Graduate

Other: _____

_____

Employment History

Date From/To	Position	Pay/Per
_____	_____	$ _____
_____	_____	$ _____
_____	_____	$ _____
_____	_____	$ _____
_____	_____	$ _____
_____	_____	$ _____

Termination Information

Date Terminated: _____ Would We Rehire? _____ Yes _____ No

Reason for Termination: _____

_____

_____

NEW EMPLOYEE DATA

Name: _____

Employee Social Security No.: _____

Address: _____

Position: _____ Department: _____

Pay frequency: _____ Pay Code: _____ Annual salary: _____

Employment Date: _____ Employment Code: _____ Cost Center: _____

Sex: _____ M _____ F

Marital Status:

_____ Single _____ Married _____ Separated _____ Widowed _____ Divorced

Birth Date: _____ Home Phone: _____

Driver's License No.: _____ State: _____ Exp. Date: _____

Spouse's Name: _____

Children

Name: _____ Birth Date: _____

Name: _____ Birth Date: _____

Name: _____ Birth Date: _____

Name: _____ Birth Date: _____

Education

High School: _____ No. of Yrs : _____ Degree: _____

College: _____ No. of Yrs : _____ Degree: _____

Post-Graduate: _____ No. of Yrs : _____ Degree: _____

Military Service: Branch _____ Rank _____ Discharge Date _____

Emergency Notification

Name: _____

Phone: _____ Relationship: _____

Address: _____

FORM N305

EMERGENCY PHONE NUMBERS

Employee: _____ Date: _____

     In the event of a medical emergency, the following people and emergency medical personnel should be contacted:

Contact 1: _____

Phone: _____

Relationship: _____

Contact 2: _____

Phone: _____

Relationship: _____

Doctor: _____

Phone: _____

Insurance Carrier & Medical Identification No.: _____

_____

Health/Medical History: _____

_____

Medication Taken and Allergies: _____

_____

Please complete and return to the Personnel Department.

EMPLOYEE HEALTH EVALUATION
(PRE-EMPLOYMENT)

Name: _____

Address: _____

Social Security No. :_____ Sex :_____ Date of Birth: _____

Physician: _____ Phone: _____

Have you ever: (Check one)

Yes   No

____ ____   1. Missed more than two weeks of work due to health or medical reasons?

____ ____   2. Been refused employment for health or medical reasons?

____ ____   3. Been awarded compensation due to an accident or injury?

____ ____   4. Been discharged from employment due to medical or health reasons?

____ ____   5. Worked with asbestos?

____ ____   6. Worked dusty jobs?

____ ____   7. Worked with radioactive materials?

Please explain all answers marked yes.

_____

_____

_____

_____

_____

Have you ever received medical treatment for: (Check one)

Yes   No

____ ____   1. Alcohol or substance abuse?

____ ____   2. A mental condition?

____ ____   3. Rheumatic fever or rheumatic heart disease?

FORM E306

_____ _____   4. Any type of cardiac disorder?

_____ _____   5. Fainting spells or seizures?

_____ _____   6. Diabetes?

_____ _____   7. Asthma, hay fever, allergies or sinus trouble?

_____ _____   8. Hepatitis or liver disease?

_____ _____   9. Stomach problems?

_____ _____   10. Ulcers?

_____ _____   11. Heart problems?

_____ _____   12. Tuberculosis?

_____ _____   13. Back problems?

_____ _____   14. Blood disorders?

Please explain answers marked yes.

_____

_____

_____

_____

_____

Other comments concerning your health

_____

_____

_____

_____

_____

_____
Signed

_____
Date

CONSENT FOR DRUG/ALCOHOL SCREENING

If you are offered and accept employment with _____ (Company) you may work with and be around machinery and equipment that can cause injury to yourself and others. In the interest of safety for all concerned, you will be required to take a urine test for drug and/or alcohol use as a condition of employment.

I, _____, have been fully informed by my potential employer of the reason for this urine test for drug and/or alcohol. I understand what I am being tested for, the procedure involved and freely give my consent. I also understand that the results of this test will be sent to my prospective employer and become part of my record.

If this test is positive, and for this reason I am not hired, I understand that I will be given the opportunity to explain the reasons for the results of this test.

I authorize these test results to be released to _____ (Company).

_____   _____
Employee   Date

_____   _____
Witness   Date

FORM C301

RECEIPT FOR COMPANY PROPERTY

Employee:_____

Identification No.: _____

Department/Section: _____

    I hereby acknowledge receipt of the company property listed below. I agree to keep the property in good condition and to return it when I terminate working for the company, or earlier on request. I agree to immediately report any loss or damage to the property. In addition, I agree to use said property only for work-related purposes.

Item:_____ Received From: _____ Date: _____

Serial No.: _____ Returned To: _____ Date: _____

Item:_____ Received From: _____ Date: _____

Serial No.: _____ Returned To: _____ Date: _____

Item:_____ Received From: _____ Date: _____

Serial No.: _____ Returned To: _____ Date: _____

Item:_____ Received From: _____ Date: _____

Serial No.: _____ Returned To: _____ Date: _____

Item:_____ Received From: _____ Date: _____

Serial No.: _____ Returned To: _____ Date: _____

Item:_____ Received From: _____ Date: _____

Serial No.: _____ Returned To: _____ Date: _____

_____
Employee

_____
Date

SAMPLES AND DOCUMENTS RECEIPT

I, _____, employed in the position of _____, confirm that I have received from my employer the following samples:

No. Rec'd.	Serial No.	Description	Value Each	Total Value
_____	_____	_____	_____	_____
_____	_____	_____	_____	_____
_____	_____	_____	_____	_____
_____	_____	_____	_____	_____
_____	_____	_____	_____	_____
_____	_____	_____	_____	_____

I further confirm that I have received the following documents:

_____

_____

_____

_____

_____

_____

I accept responsibility to safeguard these materials, prevent the disclosure of confidential material and return these (except those authorized for and delivered to customers) to my employer upon demand and, in any event, upon termination of employment.

_____
Employee

_____
Date

FORM S302

EEO ANALYSIS OF NEW HIRES

Date: _____

Job Group	Male	Minorities	Female	Total Employees	% Minority	% Female
Senior Management	____	_____	_____	_____	_____	_____
Middle Management	____	_____	_____	_____	_____	_____
Supervisors	____	_____	_____	_____	_____	_____
Professionals	____	_____	_____	_____	_____	_____
Technicians	____	_____	_____	_____	_____	_____
Sales Personnel	____	_____	_____	_____	_____	_____
Clerical Personnel	____	_____	_____	_____	_____	_____
Service Personnel	____	_____	_____	_____	_____	_____
TOTAL	____	_____	_____	_____	_____	_____

Section 4
Personnel Management

Form E401	**Employment Record** - Records an employee's positions with the company.
Form P401	**Personnel Data Change** - Records changes in an employee's address, marital status and number of dependents.
Form E402	**Employee Information Update** - Requests employees to update information for personnel file.
Form E403	**Employee Salary Record** - Records history of employee's salary and positions with company.
Form E404	**Employment Changes** - Records any changes in employee's position and salary.
Form P402	**Personnel Data Sheet** - Records changes in employee's salary and position with company.
Form P403	**Personnel File Access Log** - Records access to personnel files.
Form R401	**Request to Inspect Personnel File** - Employee form to request inspection of file.
Form C401	**Consent to Release Information** - Authorizes release of employment information.
Form T401	**Telephone Reference Record** - Records information about employee references given by telephone.
Form P404	**Personnel Activity Report** - Records the number of employees, salaries and positions during a given period.
Form P405	**Personnel Requirement Projections** - Projects personnel requirements for a given period.
Form T402	**Temporary Employment Requisition** - Requests employees for a temporary period.
Form T403	**Temporary Personnel Requisition** - Requests an employee for a temporary period.
Form E405	**Employee Flextime Schedule** - Records an employee's schedule.

Form W401	**Weekly Work Schedule** - Establishes employees' schedules for a given week.
Form D401	**Daily Time Record** - Records employees' hours for a given day.
Form E406	**Employee Daily Time Record** - Records an employee's daily hours over a specified period.
Form W402	**Weekly Time Record** - Records employees' weekly hours over a given period.
Form H401	**Hourly Employees' Weekly Time Sheet** - Records hourly employees' daily and weekly hours for a given week.
Form D402	**Department Overtime Request** - Requests a specific amount of overtime for specified employees.
Form O401	**Overtime Permit** - Authorizes a specific amount of overtime for a specific employee.
Form O402	**Overtime Authorization** - Authorizes specified overtime for a specified employee.
Form O403	**Overtime Report** - Records total hours and total salaries for a specific department during a specific payroll period.
Form D403	**Department Overtime Report** - Records employees' overtime hours in a specific department for a specific period.
Form D404	**Department Payroll** - Records employees' regular and overtime hours or wages for a specific department and period.
Form E407	**Expense Report** - Records an employee's expenses for a company trip.
Form M401	**Mileage Reimbursement Report** - Records an employee's company reimbursable mileage for a given month.
Form P406	**Payroll Change Notice** - Notifies payroll department of a change in payroll.
Form P407	**Pay Advice** - Advises payroll department of an employee's gross and net pay for a given payroll period.
Form P408	**Payroll Summary** - Summarizes an employee's deductions and gross and net pay for a given payroll period.
Form V401	**Vacation Request Memo** - Employee's request to take a specified number of vacation days.

Form V402	**Vacation Request** - Records an employee's requested vacation dates.
Form E408	**Employee Health Record** - Records an employee's illnesses and injuries that affect employment.
Form A401	**Accident Report** - Records events of an accident.
Form I401	**Illness Report** - Records an employee's illness that affects employment.
Form I402	**Injury Report** - Records an employee's injury.
Form D405	**Disability Certificate** - Certifies an employee's disability.
Form P409	**Physician's Report** - Certifies that an employee's absence is medically necessary.
Form E409	**Employee Sympathy Letter 1** - Letter to injured employee.
Form E410	**Employee Sympathy Letter 2** - Letter to ill employee.
Form E411	**Employee Sympathy Letter 3** - Letter to injured employee.
Form E412	**Employee Sympathy Letter 4** - Letter to ill employee.
Form A402	**Absence Request** - Employee's request to miss work.
Form F401	**Funeral Leave Request** - Employee's request to miss work for a funeral.
Form L401	**Leave/Return from Leave Request** - Record of employee's reason for absence.
Form M402	**Military Duty Absence** - Request for military absence.
Form L402	**Late Report** - Supervisor's report of employee's late arrival.
Form E413	**Employee Absence Report** - Record of employee's absence.
Form A403	**Absence Report** - Supervisor's report of employee's absence.
Form D406	**Department Absence Report** - Department report of employees' absences.
Form A404	**Annual Attendance Record** - Employee's annual attendance record.
Form E414	**Employee Suggestion** - Records suggestion for improving work conditions.
Form S401	**Suggestion Plan 1** - Outlines employee suggestion plan.
Form S402	**Suggestion Plan 2** - Outlines employee suggestion plan.

Form S403	**Suggestion Plan 3** - Outlines employee suggestion plan.
Form M403	**Memo Regarding Drug Testing** - Informs employees of company's policy prohibiting drug use.
Form T404	**Test Notice Polygraph** - Notifies employee of date and time of polygraph test.
Form I403	**Information Notice Polygraph** - Informs employees of company's polygraph policy.
Form N401	**Notice of Affirmative Action Policy** - Informs employees of company's affirmative action policy.
Form A405	**Affirmative Action Notice to Suppliers** - Notifies suppliers of company's affirmative action policy and requests compliance.
Form A406	**Affirmative Action Self-Identification** - Seeks identification of current or prospective employees who fit affirmative action program.
Form A407	**Affirmative Action Suppliers Compliance Certificate** - Certifies that a supplier complies with company's affirmative action policy.
Form A408	**Affirmative Action Summary** - Summarizes minority makeup of company employees.
Form E415	**Equal Employment Opportunity Policy** - Outlines company's equal employment opportunity policy.
Form C402	**Current EEO Workforce Analysis** - Analyzes company's minority makeup.
Form E416	**EEO Analysis of Promotions** - Analyzes minority makeup of employees promoted in company.
Form E417	**Employee Transfer Request** - Records employee's request for a transfer.
Form O404	**Off-Duty Employment Request** - Employee's request to earn money during off hours.
Form G401	**Grievance Form** - Tracks an employee's complaint against company policy or action.

EMPLOYMENT RECORD

Employee:_____

Employee Number:_____

Date	Department	Position	Rate	Per	Comments
_____	_____	_____	_____	___	_____
_____	_____	_____	_____	___	_____
_____	_____	_____	_____	___	_____
_____	_____	_____	_____	___	_____
_____	_____	_____	_____	___	_____
_____	_____	_____	_____	___	_____
_____	_____	_____	_____	___	_____
_____	_____	_____	_____	___	_____
_____	_____	_____	_____	___	_____
_____	_____	_____	_____	___	_____
_____	_____	_____	_____	___	_____
_____	_____	_____	_____	___	_____
_____	_____	_____	_____	___	_____
_____	_____	_____	_____	___	_____
_____	_____	_____	_____	___	_____
_____	_____	_____	_____	___	_____
_____	_____	_____	_____	___	_____
_____	_____	_____	_____	___	_____

Submitted by: _____ Date: _____

Approved by: _____ Date: _____

FORM E401

PERSONNEL DATA CHANGE

Employee:_____ Employment Date: _____

Department: _____ Supervisor: _____

Effective Date: _____ Social Security No.: _____

Change/Update Employee Personnel File as Follows:

Name (Marital) Change: _____

New Address: _____

New Telephone No.: _____

Marital Status:_____

Number of Dependents:_____

Number of Exemptions:_____

Other: _____

_____

_____

_____

_____

_____

_____

_____   _____
Employee   Date

_____   _____
Supervisor   Date

EMPLOYEE INFORMATION UPDATE

To All Employees:

Please print all information.

Name: _____

Street Address: _____

City: _____

State: _____

Zip Code: _____

Telephone Number: _____

Social Security Number: _____

Marital Status: _____

Name of Spouse: _____

Number of Dependents: _____

Emergency Contact: _____

Emergency Telephone Number: _____

FORM E402

EMPLOYEE SALARY RECORD

Employee: _____

Starting Date: _____ Starting Salary: _____

Position	Increase Date	Increase	Type of Increase (merit/promotion/ COL/etc.)
_____	_____	_____	_____
_____	_____	_____	_____
_____	_____	_____	_____
_____	_____	_____	_____
_____	_____	_____	_____
_____	_____	_____	_____
_____	_____	_____	_____
_____	_____	_____	_____
_____	_____	_____	_____
_____	_____	_____	_____
_____	_____	_____	_____
_____	_____	_____	_____
_____	_____	_____	_____
_____	_____	_____	_____
_____	_____	_____	_____
_____	_____	_____	_____
_____	_____	_____	_____
_____	_____	_____	_____
_____	_____	_____	_____

EMPLOYMENT CHANGES

Employee: _____ Employment Date: _____

Department: _____ Supervisor: _____

Effective Date: _____ Date Submitted: _____

1.   Pay Rate Change:

     From: _____ to _____

2.   Position Title Change:

     From: _____ to _____

3.   Position Classification Change:

     From: _____ to _____

4.   Shift Change:

     From: _____ to _____

5.   Full-Time/Part-Time Change:

     From: _____ to _____

6.   Temporary/Permanent Change:

     From: _____ to _____

7.   Other: (Describe)

     _____

     _____

_____   _____
Submitted By   Date

_____   _____
Approved By   Date

FORM E404

PERSONNEL DATA SHEET

Employee:_____

Employment Date: _____ Social Security No.:_____

Address: _____

_____ Phone: _____

New Address: _____

_____ Phone: _____

Emergency Contact:_____ Phone: _____

Marital Status: _____ Spouse Name: _____

Type of Personnel Change	Date	Pay Increase	Merit/Promotion/Other
_____	_____	_____	_____
_____	_____	_____	_____
_____	_____	_____	_____
_____	_____	_____	_____
_____	_____	_____	_____
_____	_____	_____	_____
_____	_____	_____	_____
_____	_____	_____	_____
_____	_____	_____	_____
_____	_____	_____	_____
_____	_____	_____	_____
_____	_____	_____	_____
_____	_____	_____	_____
_____	_____	_____	_____
_____	_____	_____	_____

PERSONNEL FILE ACCESS LOG

Employee:_____

Social Security Number: _____

THIS FILE MUST REMAIN WITH THE PERSONNEL DEPARTMENT.

Notice: All medical information, pre-employment references, current investigations in progress, and EEO data shall be removed from this file prior to any review.

Date	Name	Reason for Review

FORM P403

REQUEST TO INSPECT PERSONNEL FILE

Employee:_____ Date Requested: _____

Social Security Number:_____

Department/Location: _____

Work Phone: _____

I request an appointment with the Personnel Department for the purpose of inspecting my personnel file.

I previously reviewed my file: _____.

_____   _____
Signature   Date

File review appointment scheduled for:

Date: _____   Time: _____

Location: _____

Date File Review Completed: _____

Employee comments regarding information in the personnel file:

_____

_____

_____

_____

_____   _____
Personnel Representative   Date

_____   _____
Employee Signature   Date

Employee should complete top section of request form and forward to the Personnel Department. Place one completed copy of this form into personnel file upon completion of review.

CONSENT TO RELEASE OF INFORMATION

To:

From: Personnel Office

A request for verification of employment information has been received from:

Please check below those items for which information may be released.

_____ Salary

_____ Position

_____ Department

_____ Supervisor

_____ Health records

_____ Dates of employment

_____ Part-time/Full-time

_____ Hours worked

_____ Whether you work under a maiden name

_____ Wage attachments

_____ Reason for separation

_____ Other:

_____   _____
Employee Signature   Date

   Please return this form to the personnel office as soon as possible. Your consent on this occasion will not constitute a consent to release on future occasions.

FORM C401

TELEPHONE REFERENCE RECORD

Reference given on employee: _____

Date: _____ Time: _____

Person Inquiring: _____

Company: _____

Address: _____

_____ Phone: _____

Reason for inquiry: _____

_____

_____

Reference Summary:

_____

_____

_____

_____

_____

Specific Questions/Replies:

_____

_____

_____

_____

_____

_____

Submitted By

PERSONNEL ACTIVITY REPORT

Period from:_____ to: _____

Date prepared: _____ Prepared by: _____

	Salaried	Hourly	Part-time
# employees at start of period	_____	_____	_____
# employees at end of period	_____	_____	_____
# positions presently open	_____	_____	_____
# applicants interviewed	_____	_____	_____
# applicants hired	_____	_____	_____
% applicants hired during period	_____	_____	_____
# employees terminated	_____	_____	_____
# employees resigned	_____	_____	_____
# openings at start of period	_____	_____	_____
# openings at end of period	_____	_____	_____
Total requisitions to be filled	_____	_____	_____
Requisitions received	_____	_____	_____
Requisitions filled	_____	_____	_____
Requisitions unfilled	_____	_____	_____
Turnover rate for period	_____	_____	_____

Other: _____ _____ _____ _____

_____ _____ _____ _____

Notes: _____

_____

_____

_____

_____

FORM P404

PERSONNEL REQUIREMENT PROJECTIONS

Period from: _____ to _____

Number of personnel required at end of time period: _____

Number employed now: _____

Loss of personnel:

Retirement:_____

Death:_____

Discharge:_____

Quit:_____

Promotion:_____

Lay-Off:_____

Transfer:_____

Total personnel loss
during time period:_____

Gain of personnel:

New hires (routine):_____

Promoted in:_____

Training graduates:_____

Additional personnel required: _____

_____   _____
Submitted By   Date

TEMPORARY EMPLOYMENT REQUISITION

To:

Date:

Number of Temporary Employees Needed:_____

Position/Duties: _____

Department: _____

Supervisor: _____

Starting Dates: _____ to_____

Shift_____ to _____

Reasons for Requisition: _____

_____

_____

_____

_____

_____

Estimated Cost: _____

Budget Number: _____

Budgeted?   yes _____ no _____

_____   _____
Signed By   Date

_____   _____
Approved By   Date

Temporary personnel are not allowed employment beyond approval period or for an amount above estimated expense, unless approved in advance.

FORM T402

TEMPORARY PERSONNEL REQUISITION

Job Title:_____ Full Time:_____ Part Time: _____

Supervisor:_____ Department:_____

Dates Desired: From: _____ through _____

Hours Desired: From: _____ to _____

Reason For Hire: _____

_____

_____

_____

_____

_____

_____

Job Duties: _____

_____

_____

_____

_____

_____

_____

_____

_____   _____
Supervisor's Signature   Date

_____   _____
Approved By   Date

EMPLOYEE FLEXTIME SCHEDULE

Employee: _____ Week Ending: _____

Day	Time In	Lunch-Out	Lunch-In	Time Out	Hours/Day
Monday	_____	_____	_____	_____	_____
Tuesday	_____	_____	_____	_____	_____
Wednesday	_____	_____	_____	_____	_____
Thursday	_____	_____	_____	_____	_____
Friday	_____	_____	_____	_____	_____
Saturday	_____	_____	_____	_____	_____
Sunday	_____	_____	_____	_____	_____
Total:	_____	_____	_____	_____	_____

FORM E405

WEEKLY WORK SCHEDULE

Week Ending: _____

HOURS

Employee	Sun	Mon	Tue	Wed	Thu	Fri	Sat
_____	_____	_____	_____	_____	_____	_____	_____
_____	_____	_____	_____	_____	_____	_____	_____
_____	_____	_____	_____	_____	_____	_____	_____
_____	_____	_____	_____	_____	_____	_____	_____
_____	_____	_____	_____	_____	_____	_____	_____
_____	_____	_____	_____	_____	_____	_____	_____
_____	_____	_____	_____	_____	_____	_____	_____
_____	_____	_____	_____	_____	_____	_____	_____
_____	_____	_____	_____	_____	_____	_____	_____
_____	_____	_____	_____	_____	_____	_____	_____
_____	_____	_____	_____	_____	_____	_____	_____
_____	_____	_____	_____	_____	_____	_____	_____
_____	_____	_____	_____	_____	_____	_____	_____
_____	_____	_____	_____	_____	_____	_____	_____
_____	_____	_____	_____	_____	_____	_____	_____
_____	_____	_____	_____	_____	_____	_____	_____
_____	_____	_____	_____	_____	_____	_____	_____
_____	_____	_____	_____	_____	_____	_____	_____
_____	_____	_____	_____	_____	_____	_____	_____
_____	_____	_____	_____	_____	_____	_____	_____

DAILY TIME RECORD

Day: _____   Date: _____

Employee	Time Began	Time Ended	Overtime	Comments
_____	_____	_____	_____	_____
_____	_____	_____	_____	_____
_____	_____	_____	_____	_____
_____	_____	_____	_____	_____
_____	_____	_____	_____	_____
_____	_____	_____	_____	_____
_____	_____	_____	_____	_____
_____	_____	_____	_____	_____
_____	_____	_____	_____	_____
_____	_____	_____	_____	_____
_____	_____	_____	_____	_____
_____	_____	_____	_____	_____
_____	_____	_____	_____	_____
_____	_____	_____	_____	_____
_____	_____	_____	_____	_____
_____	_____	_____	_____	_____
_____	_____	_____	_____	_____
_____	_____	_____	_____	_____
_____	_____	_____	_____	_____

By: _____

FORM D401

EMPLOYEE DAILY TIME RECORD

Employee: _____ Period Ending:_____

Department: _____ Supervisor: _____

Date	Time Started	Time Finished	Overtime	Total
_____	_____	_____	_____	_____
_____	_____	_____	_____	_____
_____	_____	_____	_____	_____
_____	_____	_____	_____	_____
_____	_____	_____	_____	_____
_____	_____	_____	_____	_____
_____	_____	_____	_____	_____
_____	_____	_____	_____	_____
_____	_____	_____	_____	_____
_____	_____	_____	_____	_____
_____	_____	_____	_____	_____
_____	_____	_____	_____	_____
_____	_____	_____	_____	_____
_____	_____	_____	_____	_____
_____	_____	_____	_____	_____
_____	_____	_____	_____	_____
_____	_____	_____	_____	_____
_____	_____	_____	_____	_____

By: _____ Title: _____ Date:_____

WEEKLY TIME RECORD

For week ending:_____

Employee	Sun	Mon	Tue	Wed	Thu	Fri	Sat	Total
_____	_____	_____	_____	_____	_____	_____	_____	_____
_____	_____	_____	_____	_____	_____	_____	_____	_____
_____	_____	_____	_____	_____	_____	_____	_____	_____
_____	_____	_____	_____	_____	_____	_____	_____	_____
_____	_____	_____	_____	_____	_____	_____	_____	_____
_____	_____	_____	_____	_____	_____	_____	_____	_____
_____	_____	_____	_____	_____	_____	_____	_____	_____
_____	_____	_____	_____	_____	_____	_____	_____	_____
_____	_____	_____	_____	_____	_____	_____	_____	_____
_____	_____	_____	_____	_____	_____	_____	_____	_____
_____	_____	_____	_____	_____	_____	_____	_____	_____
_____	_____	_____	_____	_____	_____	_____	_____	_____
_____	_____	_____	_____	_____	_____	_____	_____	_____
_____	_____	_____	_____	_____	_____	_____	_____	_____
_____	_____	_____	_____	_____	_____	_____	_____	_____
_____	_____	_____	_____	_____	_____	_____	_____	_____
_____	_____	_____	_____	_____	_____	_____	_____	_____
_____	_____	_____	_____	_____	_____	_____	_____	_____
_____	_____	_____	_____	_____	_____	_____	_____	_____

Totals: _____ _____ _____ _____ _____ _____ _____ _____

FORM W402

HOURLY EMPLOYEES' WEEKLY TIME SHEET

Complete hours for each employee and for each day worked. Mark days not worked.

Week of: _____, 19 _____.

Employee	Sun	Mon	Tue	Wed	Thu	Fri	Sat	Total
_____	___	___	___	___	___	___	___	___
_____	___	___	___	___	___	___	___	___
_____	___	___	___	___	___	___	___	___
_____	___	___	___	___	___	___	___	___
_____	___	___	___	___	___	___	___	___
_____	___	___	___	___	___	___	___	___
_____	___	___	___	___	___	___	___	___
_____	___	___	___	___	___	___	___	___
_____	___	___	___	___	___	___	___	___
_____	___	___	___	___	___	___	___	___
_____	___	___	___	___	___	___	___	___
_____	___	___	___	___	___	___	___	___
_____	___	___	___	___	___	___	___	___
_____	___	___	___	___	___	___	___	___
_____	___	___	___	___	___	___	___	___
_____	___	___	___	___	___	___	___	___
_____	___	___	___	___	___	___	___	___
_____	___	___	___	___	___	___	___	___
Totals:	___	___	___	___	___	___	___	___

DEPARTMENT OVERTIME REQUEST

Department: _____ Date: _____

Employee	Employee ID No.	Overtime Requested	Authorized
_____	_____	_____	_____
_____	_____	_____	_____
_____	_____	_____	_____
_____	_____	_____	_____
_____	_____	_____	_____
_____	_____	_____	_____
_____	_____	_____	_____
_____	_____	_____	_____
_____	_____	_____	_____
_____	_____	_____	_____
_____	_____	_____	_____
_____	_____	_____	_____
_____	_____	_____	_____
_____	_____	_____	_____
_____	_____	_____	_____
_____	_____	_____	_____
_____	_____	_____	_____

Total: _____

Signature: _____

FORM D402

OVERTIME PERMIT

Date:

To:

Name: Department: ,

has been approved and authorized to work overtime for a maximum of   hours
between the dates of   and

, for the purpose of:

The overtime rate shall be paid in accordance with company policy.

Other comments/conditions for overtime approval:

_____   _____
Approval Requested By   Date

_____   _____
Approved By   Date

OVERTIME AUTHORIZATION

Department: _____ Date: _____

Employee: _____ Employee ID No.: _____

Overtime Hours Authorized: _____

Reason for Overtime: _____

_____

_____

_____

_____

_____

_____

_____

_____

_____

_____

_____

_____

_____

Requested by: _____

Title: _____ Date: _____

Approved by: _____

Title: _____ Date: _____

FORM O402

OVERTIME REPORT

Department: _____ Date: _____

Payroll Period	Total Hours	Total Salaries	Percent of Payroll
_____	_____	_____	_____
_____	_____	_____	_____
_____	_____	_____	_____
_____	_____	_____	_____
_____	_____	_____	_____
_____	_____	_____	_____
_____	_____	_____	_____
_____	_____	_____	_____
_____	_____	_____	_____
_____	_____	_____	_____
_____	_____	_____	_____
_____	_____	_____	_____
_____	_____	_____	_____
_____	_____	_____	_____
_____	_____	_____	_____
_____	_____	_____	_____
_____	_____	_____	_____

_____   _____
Approval Requested By   Date

_____   _____
Approved By   Date

DEPARTMENT OVERTIME REPORT

Department: _____ Time Period: _____

Supervisor: _____

Employee	Date	Overtime Hours	Overtime Paid	Percent of Payroll
_____	_____	_____	_____	_____
_____	_____	_____	_____	_____
_____	_____	_____	_____	_____
_____	_____	_____	_____	_____
_____	_____	_____	_____	_____
_____	_____	_____	_____	_____
_____	_____	_____	_____	_____
_____	_____	_____	_____	_____
_____	_____	_____	_____	_____
_____	_____	_____	_____	_____
_____	_____	_____	_____	_____
_____	_____	_____	_____	_____
_____	_____	_____	_____	_____
_____	_____	_____	_____	_____
_____	_____	_____	_____	_____

_____   _____
Submitted By   Date

_____   _____
Approved By   Date

FORM D403

DEPARTMENT PAYROLL

Period beginning:_____ Ending: _____

Employee	Hours		Pay Rate	Wages		Total Wages
	Reg	OT		Reg	OT	
_____	_____	_____	_____	_____	_____	_____
_____	_____	_____	_____	_____	_____	_____
_____	_____	_____	_____	_____	_____	_____
_____	_____	_____	_____	_____	_____	_____
_____	_____	_____	_____	_____	_____	_____
_____	_____	_____	_____	_____	_____	_____
_____	_____	_____	_____	_____	_____	_____
_____	_____	_____	_____	_____	_____	_____
_____	_____	_____	_____	_____	_____	_____
_____	_____	_____	_____	_____	_____	_____
_____	_____	_____	_____	_____	_____	_____
_____	_____	_____	_____	_____	_____	_____
_____	_____	_____	_____	_____	_____	_____
_____	_____	_____	_____	_____	_____	_____
_____	_____	_____	_____	_____	_____	_____
_____	_____	_____	_____	_____	_____	_____
_____	_____	_____	_____	_____	_____	_____
_____	_____	_____	_____	_____	_____	_____
_____	_____	_____	_____	_____	_____	_____
Totals:	_____	_____		_____	_____	_____

EXPENSE REPORT

Name:_____ Department:_____

Trip Purpose:_____ From: _____ to _____

    Attach receipts before submitting for reimbursement.

Date:_____ Total: _____

                  Expense   Place

Airfare: _____

Trainfare:_____

Car Rental:_____

Tolls: _____

Gasoline: _____

Taxi: _____

Breakfast: _____

Lunch:_____

Dinner: _____

Hotel:_____

Telephone: _____

Other: _____

Total: $ _____

Amount Advanced: $ _____

Net Due: $ _____

I hereby affirm that the above expenses are true and accurate.

_____   _____

Signed   Approved By

Dept:_____   Title: _____

Date: _____   Date: _____

FORM E407

MILEAGE REIMBURSEMENT REPORT

Employee: _____

Driver's License No.: _____ Registration No.:_____

Type of Vehicle: _____

Department:_____ Month: _____

Date	Beginning Reading	Ending Reading	Total Mileage	Reason for Travel
_____	_____	_____	_____	_____
_____	_____	_____	_____	_____
_____	_____	_____	_____	_____
_____	_____	_____	_____	_____
_____	_____	_____	_____	_____
_____	_____	_____	_____	_____
_____	_____	_____	_____	_____
_____	_____	_____	_____	_____
_____	_____	_____	_____	_____
_____	_____	_____	_____	_____
_____	_____	_____	_____	_____
_____	_____	_____	_____	_____
_____	_____	_____	_____	_____
_____	_____	_____	_____	_____

Total mileage this month:_____ @ $ 0._____Per Mile = $_____

_____   _____
Approved By   Date

Title: _____

PAYROLL CHANGE NOTICE

Date: _____   Effective Date: _____

_____ Enter on Payroll   _____ Promotion

_____ Change Rate   _____ Discharged

_____ Transfer to _____   _____ Temp. Layoff

_____ Remove from Payroll   _____ Raise

_____ Quit   _____   _____

_____ Terminated

Employee: _____

Employee Number: _____

Social Security No.: _____

Old Rate: _____

New Rate: _____

Comments: _____

_____

_____   _____
Submitted By   Date

_____   _____
Approved By   Date

FORM P406

PAY ADVICE

Employee: _____ Date: _____

Employee ID No.: _____

Social Security No.: _____

Payments	Hours	Rate	Total
Regular:	_____	_____	_____
Overtime:	_____	_____	_____
Vacation:	_____	_____	_____

Gross Payable: _____

Deductions

Social Security (FICA): _____

Unemployment Insurance: _____

Federal Withholding Tax: _____

State Withholding Tax: _____

Local Withholding Tax: _____

_____

Total Deductions: _____

Net Payable: _____

Keep this record of your earnings

PAYROLL SUMMARY

Employee:_____

Social Security No.: _____   Employee ID No.: _____

Department: _____   Payroll Period Ending:_____

Gross Pay: $ _____

Deductions

    Federal Withholding:_____

    State Withholding:_____

    FICA:_____

    Insurance:_____

    Pension Plan:_____

    Dues:_____

    401K:_____

    Other:_____

    _____

Total Deductions:_____

Net Pay:_____

Prepared By: _____   Date: _____

FORM P408

VACATION REQUEST MEMO

MEMO TO: Payroll Department

    I request permission to take   days of vacation from to   . These days are unearned and I agree that if I quit before this vacation time is earned, the company may withhold the unearned pay from my final check.

_____   _____
Employee   Date

_____   _____
Supervisor   Date

VACATION REQUEST

Employee: _____ Employment Date:_____

I request a ____ week vacation:

    From : _____ through _____

My alternate choice is:

    From: _____ through _____

(if a holiday occurs during your vacation, please request extra days below.)

_____

_____

_____

I prefer to split my vacation:

    First Week: From: _____ through _____

    Second Week: From: _____ through _____

    Third Week: From: _____ through _____

    Fourth Week: From: _____ through _____

Below vacation dates approved by: _____

Date:_____

Approved vacation dates: _____

EMPLOYEE HEALTH RECORD

Name: _____

Address: _____

_____ Phone: _____

Date Employed: _____ Position: _____

Sex: _____ Age: _____ Date of Pre-Employment Exam: _____

Physician: _____ Phone: _____

Medical History (Allergies, Restrictions, Etc.):_____

_____

_____

_____

In Emergency, Notify:_____ Relationship: _____

Address: _____

_____ Phone: _____

Date	Time	Illness/Injury	Treatment/Action
_____	_____	_____	_____
_____	_____	_____	_____
_____	_____	_____	_____
_____	_____	_____	_____
_____	_____	_____	_____
_____	_____	_____	_____
_____	_____	_____	_____
_____	_____	_____	_____

_____   _____
Employee Signature   Date

ACCIDENT REPORT

Employee: _____ Age: _____ Sex: _____

Department: _____ Supervisor: _____

Date of accident: _____

Nature of injuries: _____

_____

_____

Cause of Accident: _____

_____

_____

If employee left work, time of leaving: _____

If employee returned to work, time of return: _____

Name and address of physician: _____

_____

If hospitalized, name and address of hospital: _____

_____

Actions undertaken to avoid similar incidents: _____

_____

_____

Comments: _____

_____

_____

_____

_____   _____
Supervisor   Date

FORM A401

ILLNESS REPORT

Employee:_____ Date:_____

Age: _____ Sex:_____

Department: _____ Supervisor: _____

Is illness related to employment? Yes (   ) No (   )

Date of diagnosis: _____

Describe illness:

_____

_____

_____

If employee left work, time of leaving: _____

If employee returned to work, time of return: _____

Name and address of physician:_____

_____

If hospitalized, name and address of hospital: _____

_____

Comments: _____

_____

_____

_____

_____

_____

_____   _____
Supervisor   Date

INJURY REPORT

Name:_____ Social Security No: _____

Address: _____

_____ Phone: _____

Age:_____ Sex: _____

Is injury related to employment?   Yes (   ) No (   )

Describe: _____

Date of injury: _____ Time of injury: _____

Date of initial diagnosis: _____

Describe the injury in detail and indicate the part of the body affected:

_____

Did employee return to work? Yes (   ) No (   ) If no, indicate last day worked:

_____

Name and address of physician: _____

_____

If hospitalized, name and address of hospital:_____

_____

Names of witnesses: _____

_____

Comments: _____

_____

_____

_____   _____
Employee   Date

_____   _____
Supervisor or first aid person   Date

FORM I402

DISABILITY CERTIFICATE

To be completed by employee:

Employee: _____

Address: _____

_____ Phone: _____

I authorize the physician to release necessary information to the below company regarding my condition while under his/her care.

_____   _____

Employee's Signature   Date

To be completed by attending physician:

Date disability began: _____

Expected return to work date: _____

Nature of disability: _____

_____

Special complications: _____

Work restrictions: _____

_____

Date(s) seen: _____

If hospitalized, name of hospital: _____

Dates: From_____ to _____

Date of surgery, if any: _____ Procedure: _____

If pregnancy, expected date of delivery: _____

Physician's name: _____

_____   _____

Physician's Signature   Date

Address: _____

_____ Phone: _____

Return to: (Company) _____

_____

_____

PHYSICIAN'S REPORT

Date:

To Dr.

Re:

Dear Doctor:

    The above named employee has been absent from work from
to   and we have been advised that our employee has been under
your medical care.

    Since we verify protracted medical absences, we would appreciate your completing
this form and returning it for our records.

Very truly,

_____

Physician's Report

    I certify that   has been under my
medical care and that the absences listed
above were medically necessary or reasonable based on the medical condition.

_____   _____
Physician   Date

FORM P409

Date:

To:

Dear   :

    The accident that has put you in the hospital was most unfortunate, and I was sorry to hear about it. Luckily the injuries do not seem to be serious. My sympathies are certainly with you.

    Your duties have been assigned to your coworkers, and needless to say, all of us miss you.

    We will all be very happy to see you back at your desk when you are well and ready to return.

                    Sincerely yours,

                    _____

Date:

To:

Dear   :

I was terribly sorry to learn you are in the hospital. I understand it is not too serious and you will be back home soon.

Please accept my best wishes for a speedy recovery. I hope you are back at your desk in the shortest time possible.

You are very much in the thoughts of all of us here, and we all hope to see you soon.

Sincerely yours,

_____

EMPLOYEE SYMPATHY LETTER 2 – FORM E410

Date:

To:

Dear   :

    I just heard about your accident, and I hope you will have started to feel better by the time this letter reaches you.

    Everyone here is thinking about you, and sends their wishes for your speedy recovery.

    In the meantime, please call if there is anything we can do for either you or your family.

                        Sincerely yours,

_____

Date:

To:

Dear   :

told me this morning that you are ill. I hope you will be feeling much better by the time this reaches you.

Everyone at the office misses you, but we hope you will take your time coming back and be sure your recovery is complete.

Best wishes from all of us.

Sincerely yours,

_____

ABSENCE REQUEST

Employee: _____ Date: _____

Department: _____

Date(s) Requested: From:_____ to_____

Hours Requested: From: _____ to_____

With Pay ( )   Without Pay ( )   Makeup ( )

Reason for Absence: _____

_____

_____

_____

_____

_____

_____

_____

_____

        Approved ( )   Not Approved ( )

Supervisor Comments:_____

_____

_____

_____

_____

_____   _____

Employee   Date

_____   _____

Supervisor   Date

FUNERAL LEAVE REQUEST

Employee: _____ Date: _____

Department: _____

Dates of missed work days: _____ Hourly Rate: _____

Name of Deceased: _____ Funeral Date: _____

Residence (city/town): _____ State: _____

Burial Place: _____

Relationship to employee: (be specific) _____

_____

_____

Comments: _____

_____

_____

_____

Employee

Approved

_____

Supervisor

FORM F401

LEAVE/RETURN FROM LEAVE REQUEST

Employee: _____ Date: _____

Position: _____ Date Hired: _____

Leave Request

Reason for Leave:

_____ Personal Disability

_____ Military

_____ Training Conference

_____ Compensatory Time Off

_____ Jury Duty

_____ Family Illness (Name)_____

_____ Family Death (Name) _____

_____ Other (Explain)_____

_____   _____

_____   _____

Leave Requested:

From: Date:_____ Time:_____ Total Hours: _____

To: Date: _____ Time:_____ Total Days: _____

Regular work schedule: _____

_____   _____
Employee   Date

Return From Leave

Absent From: Date: _____ Time: _____ Total Hours: _____

To: Date:_____ Time: _____ Total Days: _____

_____ Excused/Warranted

_____ Not Excused/Not Warranted (Explain) _____

_____ Resumed Part-Time Work

_____ Resumed Full-Time Work

_____ Resumed Modified Duty (Explain) _____

_____ Other (Explain)_____

Affirmed By: _____ Date: _____

MILITARY DUTY ABSENCE

Date:

To:

     I hereby request absence or leave from my employment for purposes of temporary active military duty from   to
, 19   .

     I certify that I am a member of the:

     I understand that if my military base pay for this period is less than my regular salary, I will be reimbursed for the difference for a period not to exceed two work weeks (10 days). I agree to furnish you a copy of my military pay statement immediately upon receipt with adjustments in salary to be made from my next paycheck.

     Furthermore, I agree to furnish the company a copy of my orders to report for service or such other appropriate certification of duty as the company may require.

_____
Employee

LATE REPORT

Employee:_____

Date: _____

Department: _____

Time Due at Work:_____ Arrival Time: _____ Time Missed: _____

Did Employee Notify Company? Yes (   )   No (   )

Reason for Tardiness: _____

_____

_____

_____

_____

_____

Action Taken:

_____ None

_____ Deduct Pay

_____ Make-Up

_____ Warning

_____ Terminate

_____ Other:_____

Comments: _____

_____

_____

_____

_____

_____   _____
Signed   Date

Title: _____

EMPLOYEE ABSENCE REPORT

Employee: _____ Date: _____

Report received by: _____

Expected # of days absent: _____ Expected date of return: _____

Time of report: _____

Absence reported to: _____

Reported by (   ) Self   (   ) Other relative

               (   ) Spouse   (   ) Friend

               (   ) Supervisor   (   ) Other: _____

Reason

               (   ) Illness   (   ) Illness in family

               (   ) Injury on job   (   ) Outside injury

               (   ) Transportation   (   ) Death in family

               (   ) Jury duty   (   ) Military duty

               (   ) Other: _____

_____

_____

_____

Signed

Comments: _____

_____

_____

_____

_____

_____

FORM F413

ABSENCE REPORT

Employee: _____ Date: _____

Department: _____

Date(s) Absent: _____ Date Return: _____ Day(s) Missed: _____

Did employee notify company in advance?   Yes (   )   No (   )

Reason for Absence: _____

_____

_____

Was Absence Approved?   Yes (   )   No (   )

Reason for Non-Notification: _____

_____

_____

Action Taken:

_____ None

_____ Deduct Pay

_____ Make-Up

_____ Warning

_____ Terminate

_____ Other: _____

Comments: _____

_____

_____

_____

_____   _____
Signed   Date

Title: _____

DEPARTMENT ABSENCE REPORT

Department: _____ Date: _____

The following employees were absent from work today:

Employee	Reason for absence	Paid/Unpaid
_____	_____	_____
_____	_____	_____
_____	_____	_____
_____	_____	_____
_____	_____	_____
_____	_____	_____
_____	_____	_____
_____	_____	_____
_____	_____	_____
_____	_____	_____
_____	_____	_____
_____	_____	_____
_____	_____	_____
_____	_____	_____
_____	_____	_____
_____	_____	_____
_____	_____	_____

_____
Signed

FORM D406

ANNUAL ATTENDANCE RECORD
FOR CALENDAR YEAR_____

Employee: _____ Social Security No.: _____
Position:_____ Department: _____

Day	Jan	Feb	Mar	Apr	May	Jun	Jul	Aug	Sep	Oct	Nov	Dec
1												
2												
3												
4												
5												
6												
7												
8												
9												
10												
11												
12												
13												
14												
15												
16												
17												
18												
19												
20												
21												
22												
23												
24												
25												
26												
27												
28												
29												
30												
31												

A = Absent   O = Other   H = Holiday   P = Personal Leave Approved
S = Sick   T = Tardy   F = Funeral Leave U = Unauthorized Absence
J = Jury Duty   I = Job Injury V = Vacation   LO = Leave of Absence

Comments and summary of attendance: _____
_____
_____

EMPLOYEE SUGGESTION

Employee: _____ Position: _____

Department: _____ Phone No.: _____

Is this a group submittal? Yes (   )   No (   )

(If yes, list all members of this group here, and obtain their signatures on the reverse side.)

_____

_____

_____

_____

What is the problem? Be specific.

_____

_____

_____

_____

What do you propose to improve this situation or problem? Be specific. Attach samples if applicable.

_____

_____

_____

_____

What benefits, savings and implementation costs can be expected from this solution? How did you calculate this savings?

_____

_____

_____

_____

I have read and understand the rules and regulations governing the Suggestion System and agree to be bound by them. I understand that the company has the sole discretion to make an award or not, and that it may use a suggestion without giving an award.

_____   _____
Employee   Date

FORM E414

SUGGESTION PLAN 1

Suggestion boxes are strategically placed throughout the company. These boxes contain suggestion forms to fill out when you have an idea you think has merit.

The idea may reduce costs, improve the quality of our products, or positively change a method. It may eliminate a dangerous hazard, reduce waste, change a handling procedure or improve housekeeping.

If approved, suggestions may receive awards according to the value of the idea. The suggestions are held on file for seven years, after which time they are void.

The Suggestion Plan allows you to express your interest, ingenuity, and initiative. We hope you use it frequently. Fill out a suggestion blank and put it in the office mail. Your idea will receive prompt acknowledgement and investigation and, we hope, approval and an award.

Sincerely,

_____

Suggestion Office

SUGGESTION PLAN 2

Make your suggestion and drop it into the suggestion box nearest you. Be sure to include your name and department.

For each company-improving idea you submit, you will earn $10.

Sincerely,

_____

Suggestion Office

SUGGESTION PLAN 3

The company Suggestion Plan enables you to make any suggestions for the benefit of everyone.

Give your suggestion to your immediate supervisor, who will see that it gets to the Evaluating Committee.

Your suggestion can help eliminate unnecessary expenses and squeeze more value out of every overhead dollar.

If the Evaluating Committee accepts your suggestion, you will be rewarded based on the suggestion's value to the company.

Look around the workplace. Review each procedure and routine in your daily tasks. Ask yourself: Is there a more cost-efficient way of doing this work? Is there a way to streamline this job? Is there a way to improve quality and accuracy? If you think so, submit your idea. We need your suggestions.

Sincerely,

_____

Suggestion Office

MEMO REGARDING DRUG TESTING

To: All Employees

From: Personnel

Subject: Drug Testing

Our company has a comprehensive policy against the use, sale, or possession of illegal drugs on company property. We intend to strictly enforce this policy.

We have strong reason to believe that some employees are using drugs at work. While we hope this is not the case, we want to advise all employees that we plan to carry out a thorough investigation of any suspected drug use or sale on our property. Our investigation may include drug testing through urinalysis and/or the use of undercover detectives.

We certainly don't want to use such drastic measures, but we will have no choice if we find reasonable evidence of drug activity.

We believe there are better ways to overcome drug abuse than investigation and prosecution. Therefore, we have contracted with an outside Employee Assistance Program (EAP). You can call on this program if you need help; the company will pay for treatment as long as you stay with the program and stay off drugs. Getting into this confidential program may save your job and your life. Call _____.

_____
Signed

TEST NOTICE - POLYGRAPH

Date:

To:

You are hereby notified that you are scheduled for a polygraph test to take place at
_____ , on _____ , 19 ___ ,
at _____ . m.

You have the right to consult with legal counsel or an employee representative before each phase of the test. However, the legal counsel or representative will not be allowed to be present in the room where the examination is administered during the actual test phase.

Attached to this notice is a complete list of questions you will be asked during the polygraph test. Please review it prior to attending the testing session. You have the right to terminate the test at any time.

The characteristics of the test and the instruments involved are:

You will receive further written information, which will be read to you before the polygraph examination.

_____
Supervisor

INFORMATION NOTICE - POLYGRAPH

Please be advised that the Employee Polygraph Protection Act and Department of Labor regulations require that you be given the following information before taking a polygraph examination:

1. (a) The polygraph examination area does____ does not____ contain a two-way mirror, a camera, and/or other devices through which you may be observed.

    (b) Another device, such as those used in conversation or recording, (will) (will not) be used during the examination.

    (c) Both you and the employer have the right, with the other's knowledge, to record electronically the entire examination.

2. (a) You have the right to terminate the test at any time.

    (b) You have the right, and shall be given the opportunity, to review all questions to be asked during the test.

    (c) You may not be asked questions in a manner that degrades or needlessly intrudes.

    (d) You may not be asked any questions concerning: Religious beliefs or opinions; beliefs regarding racial matters; political beliefs or affiliations; matters relating to sexual behavior; beliefs, affiliations, opinions, or lawful activities regarding unions or labor organizations.

    (e) The test may not be conducted if there is sufficient written evidence by a physician that you are suffering from a medical or psychological condition or undergoing treatment that might cause abnormal responses during the examination.

3. (a) The test is not and cannot be required as a condition of employment.

    (b) The employer may not discharge, dismiss, discipline, deny employment or promotion, or otherwise discriminate against you based solely on the analysis of a polygraph test, or based on your refusal to take such a test, without additional evidence that would support such action.

    (c) (1) In connection with an ongoing investigation, the additional evidence required for an employer to take adverse action against you, including termination, may be (A) evidence that you had access to the property that is the subject of investigation, and (B) evidence supporting the employer's reasonable suspicion that you were involved in the incident or activity under investigation.

    (2) Any statement made by you before or during the test may serve as additional supporting evidence for an adverse employment action, as described in 3(b) above, and any admission of criminal conduct by you may be transmitted to an appropriate government law enforcement agency.

FORM I403

4. (a) Information acquired from a polygraph test may be disclosed by the examiner or by the employer only:

    (1) To you or any other person specifically authorized in writing by you to receive such information;

    (2) To the employer who requested the test;

    (3) To a court, governmental agency, arbitrator or mediator that obtains a court order;

    (4) To a U.S. Department of Labor official when specifically designated in writing by you to receive such information.

    (b) Information acquired from a polygraph test may be disclosed by the employer to an appropriate governmental agency without a court order where, and only insofar as, the information disclosed is an admission of criminal conduct.

5. If any of your rights or protections under the law are violated, you have the right to file a complaint with the Wage and Hour Division of the U.S. Department of Labor, or to take action in court against the employer. Employers who violate this law are liable to the affected examinee, who may recover such legal or equitable relief as may be appropriate, including employment, reinstatement and promotion, payment of lost wages and benefits, and reasonable costs, including attorney's fees. The Secretary of Labor may also bring action to restrain violations of the Act or may assess civil money penalties against the employer.

6. Your rights under the Act may not be waived, either voluntarily or involuntarily, by contract or otherwise, except as part of a written settlement to a pending action or complaint under the Act, and agreed to and signed by the parties.

I, the undersigned, acknowledge that I have received a copy of the above notice, and that it has been read to me.

_____   _____
Signature   Date

_____
Print Name

NOTICE OF AFFIRMATIVE ACTION POLICY

Date:

To:

Our organization wants to fulfill its role as an equal opportunity employer. We request your support in our affirmative action efforts as it relates to providing employment opportunity for minority groups and women. It is our policy not to discriminate against any employee or applicant for employment because of age, race, sex, creed, color, religion, national origin, veteran or handicapped status.

The use of any agency is conditioned upon their full compliance with our equal employment opportunity policy. We request that qualified women and minorities be referred to us for any job opening we have listed with your agency.

We truly appreciate your support of our commitment to equal employment opportunity. Thank you.

Sincerely,

_____

Personnel Manager

AFFIRMATIVE ACTION NOTICE TO SUPPLIERS

Date:

To:

Re: Compliance Certificate

Our organization, as a federal government contractor, has taken affirmative action to equal employment opportunity, elimination of segregated facilities, and has filed an Affirmative Action Plan with the Department of Labor describing its efforts toward said objectives. Both federal law and the Affirmative Action Plan require that all suppliers providing goods and services to organizations such as ours agree to the provisions of the Presidential Executive Order No. 11246, dated September 24, 1981.

According to our records, you have provided goods and services to us, and, therefore, we request that you indicate your compliance with the provisions of Executive Order No. 11246 by signing the enclosed Compliance Certificate and returning it to us.

By signing and returning the enclosed certificate, you will indicate your firm's acceptance and compliance with this program for a period of one (1) year. It is our desire to complete our records as soon as possible. Your cooperation is greatly appreciated.

Sincerely,

_____
Personnel Manager

Enclosure

AFFIRMATIVE ACTION SELF-IDENTIFICATION

Date:

To: All Employees/Applicants

Our organization will take affirmative action to employ, and advance in employment, qualified Special Disabled Veterans, Veterans of the Vietnam Era, and handicapped individuals at all levels.

If you qualify, and would like to participate in the affirmative action program, please contact the undersigned. It would be helpful if you notified us of (1) your qualifications, special skills or procedures that may better enable you to perform in your present job or in any position in which you are interested, and (2) any reasonable accommodation we could make that would enable you to perform the job properly and safely. In an effort to advance employment opportunities for handicapped individuals and Vietnam Era/Special Disabled Veterans, reasonable accommodation will be provided whenever possible.

This is a voluntary program and refusal to provide this information will not subject you to discharge or disciplinary treatment. The information submitted by you will be kept confidential except that (1) management may be notified of restrictions on the work duties of special disabled veterans or handicapped individuals, and regarding necessary accommodations, (2) medical and safety personnel may be notified when and where necessary, and (3) government officials investigating compliance with the Act shall be notified. An individual may notify the company of his/her desire to benefit under this program at any future time.

Sincerely,

_____
EEO Administrator

FORM A406

AFFIRMATIVE ACTION
SUPPLIERS COMPLIANCE CERTIFICATE

Seller Name: _____ Phone: _____

Address: _____

Number of Employees: _____

This Firm is:

(   ) Independently Owned and Operated

or

(   ) An Affiliate of

or   Parent Company: _____

(   ) A Subsidiary of

or   Address:_____

(   ) A Division of

                                                      _____

Seller   Seller
Has   Has Not

_____ _____   Held contracts or subcontracts subject to the Equal Opportunity Clause
               of Executive Order 11246.

_____ _____   Filed the Equal Employment Opportunity information report EEO-1 for
               the period ending March 31 prior.

_____ _____   Filed Equal Employment Opportunity information report EEO-1 when
               required.

_____ _____   Developed a written Affirmative Action Program.

     Seller's Equal Employment Opportunity Program has/has not been subjected to a
Government Equal Opportunity Compliance Review.

     If so, when? _____.

Seller acknowledges receipt of the notice to prospective subcontractors of requirement for
certification of nonsegregated facilities and certifies/ does not certify compliance with that
requirement.

_____   _____
Signature/Title   Date

Please return to:

AFFIRMATIVE ACTION SUMMARY

Date: from _____ to: _____

	White	Black	Hispanic	Asian	American Indian
Female applicants for hire:	____	____	____	____	____
Number hired:	____	____	____	____	____
Female applicants for promotion:	____	____	____	____	____
Promotions:	____	____	____	____	____
Terminations:	____	____	____	____	____

	White	Black	Hispanic	Asian	American Indian
Male applicants for hire:	____	____	____	____	____
Number hired:	____	____	____	____	____
Male applicants for promotion:	____	____	____	____	____
Promotions:	____	____	____	____	____
Terminations:	____	____	____	____	____

FORM A408

EQUAL EMPLOYMENT OPPORTUNITY POLICY

It is the ongoing policy of our company to afford equal employment opportunity to qualified individuals regardless of their race, color, religion, sex, national origin, age, physical or mental handicap, veteran status, or because they are disabled veterans, and to conform to applicable laws and regulations. In keeping with the intent of this policy, the company will adhere strictly to the following personnel practices:

Recruitment, hiring, and promotion of individuals in all job classifications will be conducted without regard to race, color, religion, national origin, age, sex, physical or mental handicap, veteran status, or because he or she is a disabled veteran, except where a bona fide occupational qualification must be met.

Employment decisions will be made in such a manner as to further the principles of equal employment opportunity through the use of valid job-related criteria.

All other personnel actions, such as compensation, benefits, transfers, training and development, educational assistance, and social and recreational programs, will be administered without regard to race, color, religion, national origin, age, sex, physical or mental handicap, veteran status, or because he or she is a disabled veteran, except where a bon fide occupational qualification must be met.

Thorough and documented analyses of all personnel actions will be conducted to ensure compliance with the concept of equal opportunity.

Overall responsibility for the development and execution of our Affirmative Action Program is delegated to _____ as EEO/AAP Coordinator. The EEO/AAP Coordinator will provide me with quarterly and special activity and progress reports.

_____   _____
President   Date

CURRENT EEO WORKFORCE ANALYSIS

Job Group	Male	Minorities	Female	Total Employees	% Minority	% Female
Senior Management:	_____	_____	_____	_____	_____	_____
Middle Management:	_____	_____	_____	_____	_____	_____
Supervisors:	_____	_____	_____	_____	_____	_____
Professionals:	_____	_____	_____	_____	_____	_____
Technicians:	_____	_____	_____	_____	_____	_____
Sales Personnel:	_____	_____	_____	_____	_____	_____
Clerical Personnel:	_____	_____	_____	_____	_____	_____
Service Personnel:	_____	_____	_____	_____	_____	_____
Total:	_____	_____	_____	_____	_____	_____

FORM C402

EEO ANALYSIS OF PROMOTIONS

Job Group	Male	Minorities	Female	Total Employees	% Minority	% Female
Senior Management:	_____	_____	_____	_____	_____	_____
Middle Management:	_____	_____	_____	_____	_____	_____
Supervisors:	_____	_____	_____	_____	_____	_____
Professionals:	_____	_____	_____	_____	_____	_____
Technicians:	_____	_____	_____	_____	_____	_____
Sales Personnel:	_____	_____	_____	_____	_____	_____
Clerical Personnel:	_____	_____	_____	_____	_____	_____
Service Personnel:	_____	_____	_____	_____	_____	_____
Total:	_____	_____	_____	_____	_____	_____

EMPLOYEE TRANSFER REQUEST

Employee:_____ Supervisor: _____

Department:_____ Shift: _____

Present Position:_____ Starting Date:_____

Requested Position: _____

Related Experience: _____

Reason for transfer request: _____

_____

_____

_____   _____
Employee   Date

Supervisor's Comments

Evaluation in present position:_____

_____

_____

Recommended action: _____

_____   _____
Supervisor   Date

Action Taken

Date received:_____ Date interviewed: _____ Time: _____

Comments: _____

_____

Action: _____

Date employee notified:_____

_____   _____
Interviewer Signature   Date

FORM E417

OFF-DUTY EMPLOYMENT REQUEST

Employee: _____ Date: _____

Dept/Div: _____ Position: _____

Outside employer or company: _____

Address: _____

_____ Phone: _____

Work days and hours/week: _____

Duration of employment: _____

Position and duties to be performed: _____

_____

_____

_____

_____

_____   _____
Employee Signature   Date

_____   _____
Supervisor Signature   Date

Approved (   )   Disapproved (   )

GRIEVANCE FORM

Employee: _____ Date: _____

Department: _____

State your grievance in detail, including the date of aggrieved act(s):

_____

_____

_____

Identify other employees with personal knowledge or observance of your grievance:

_____

_____

_____

State briefly your efforts to resolve this grievance: _____

_____

_____

_____

Describe the remedy or solution you seek: _____

_____

_____

_____

_____   _____
Employee   Date

FORM G401

Grievance Team Personnel - Informal Review   Date Received: _____

Actions Taken: _____

_____

Disposition: _____

Employee Grievance Accepted: _____ Employee Appealed: _____

Assigned Team Member: _____

Date Communicated:_____

Grievance Team - Formal Review   Date Received: _____

Actions Taken: _____

_____

Disposition: _____

Employee Grievance Accepted: _____ Employee Appealed: _____

Grievance Review Team: _____

Date Communicated:_____

Grievance Team and Management-Formal Review   Date Received:_____

Actions Taken: _____

_____

Disposition: _____

Employee Grievance Accepted: _____ Employee Appealed: _____

Grievance Review Team: _____

Date Communicated:_____

Section 5
Performance Evaluation

Form E501	**Employee Consultation** – Records information about a consultation with employee.
Form E502	**Employee Counseling Activity Sheet** – Records information about a counseling session with employee.
Form C501	**Critical Incidents Report** – Records information about an incident requiring disciplinary action.
Form I501	**Incident Report** – Records information about an incident requiring disciplinary action.
Form N501	**Notice of Ongoing Investigation - Polygraph** – Notifies an employee to submit to a polygraph test as a result of investigation into a specific incident.
Form N502	**Notice of 30-Day Evaluation** – Notifies employee of the need to improve performance or face termination.
Form N503	**Notice of Probation** – Notifies employee to improve performance.
Form N504	**Notice of Extended Probation** – Notifies employee that probation has been extended.
Form E503	**Excessive Absenteeism Warning** – Warns employee of excessive absenteeism.
Form F501	**First Warning Notice** – First notice to employee regarding need to improve performance.
Form S501	**Second Warning Notice** – Second notice to employee regarding need to improve performance.
Form D501	**Disciplinary Notice** – Notice to employee of consequences faced if performance isn't improved.
Form D502	**Disciplinary Warning** – Warns employee of company's next action if performance isn't improved.
Form D503	**Disciplinary Report** – Records disciplinary action taken for an employee's poor performance.
Form S502	**Suspension Without Pay Notice** – Notifies employee of suspension without pay.

Form E504	**Employee Self-Evaluation** – Employee's evaluation of his/her own job performance.
Form P501	**Performance Analysis Employee Worksheet** – Analyzes employee's own job performance.
Form E505	**Employee Performance Checklist** – Supervisor's list of employee skills and qualities being rated.
Form N505	**New Employee Evaluation** – Supervisor's evaluation of new employee's job performance.
Form M501	**Managerial Evaluation** – Supervisor's evaluation of employee as management material.
Form P502	**Performance Evaluation** – Employee job performance evaluation.
Form P503	**Production Personnel Evaluation** – Evaluation of production personnel.
Form S503	**Sales Personnel Evaluation** – Evaluation of sales personnel.
Form S504	**Standard Evaluation** – Standard evaluation form.
Form T501	**Temporary Employee Evaluation** – Evaluation of temporary employee.
Form E506	**Employee Performance Review** – Shows areas employee can improve performance.
Form P504	**Performance Appraisal Interview Report** – Records results of an employee's performance appraisal interview.
Form E507	**Employee Rating Response** – Records employee's response to supervisor's evaluation.
Form P505	**Performance Objectives** – Establishes objectives for performance.
Form C502	**Coaching Form** – Outlines employee's strengths and weaknesses.
Form E508	**Employee Performance Improvement Plan** – Outlines employee's action to correct performance.
Form L501	**Letter of Commendation** – Letter commending employee on performance.
Form S505	**Salary Change Request** – Records salary increase recommendation.

EMPLOYEE CONSULTATION

Employee: _____ Department: _____

Nature of Problem: _____

Date of Problem: _____

Warning: First (   )   Second (   )   Third (   )

Suspension: From:_____ to_____ Return to Work:_____

Discharge:_____

Description of Problem: _____

_____

_____

_____

_____

Disciplinary action to be taken: _____

_____

_____

_____

_____

Employee Statement: _____

_____

_____

_____

_____   _____

Supervisor   Date

_____   _____

Employee   Date

FORM E501

EMPLOYEE COUNSELING ACTIVITY SHEET

Employee: _____ Date: _____

Time in: _____ Time out: _____

Employee relations staff member: _____

Please check one of the following:

_____ Career planning

_____ Compensation/Benefits

_____ Job posting

_____ EEO/AA

_____ Disciplinary problems

_____ Other: _____

Briefly state the problem: _____

_____

_____

_____

Necessary follow-up sessions:

_____

_____

_____

Results/Solution or outcome of session(s): _____

_____

_____

_____

_____
Supervisor

CRITICAL INCIDENTS REPORT

Employee: _____ Date: _____

Incident: _____

_____

_____

_____

_____

Employee's action: _____

_____

_____

_____

_____

Supervisor's appraisal:_____

_____

_____

_____

_____

Disciplinary action taken: _____

_____

_____

_____

_____

_____

Supervisor's Signature

FORM C501

INCIDENT REPORT

Employee: _____ Date: _____

Department: _____ Supervisor: _____

Date of incident: _____

Describe incident: _____

_____

_____

_____

Action taken: _____

_____

_____

_____

Witnesses:

Name   Address

_____   _____

_____   _____

_____   _____

_____   _____

Reported to:

Person   Date

_____   _____

_____   _____

_____   _____

Use reverse side for additional remarks.

NOTICE OF ONGOING INVESTIGATION - POLYGRAPH

Date:

To:

An ongoing investigation is being conducted of a specific incident or activity which resulted in financial loss or injury to the company. Pursuant to that investigation, you are hereby requested to submit to a polygraph test.

Since you had access to the property that is the subject of the investigation, there is a reasonable basis for suspicion that you were involved in the incident or activity under investigation.

The specific incident or activity being investigated involves:

The company suffered the following financial loss or injury as a result of this incident or activity:

You had the following access to the property that is the subject of the investigation:

The following is the basis for the reasonable suspicion that you were involved in the incident or activity under investigation:

You will receive separate written notice concerning the schedule of the polygraph test.

_____

FORM N501

NOTICE OF 30-DAY EVALUATION

Date:

To:

As a result of your failure to correct the problem described below, even after oral discussions and a written warning, you are now being placed on a 30-day formal evaluation, effective _____ , 19 _____ .

As we discussed earlier, the problem with your performance is:

The targets we agreed upon for your period of evaluation are:

I have scheduled a counseling session on _____ , 19 _____ , to meet with you and go over your progress during this period. Please be assured that I will be available for discussions and counseling at any time during this evaluation. I truly hope this action will result in positive improvement. Failure to correct this situation, however, will result in your termination, either at the end of the evaluation period, or before that time if no improvement is evident.

_____   _____
Supervisor   Date

_____   _____
Supervisor's Manager   Date

_____   _____
Employee   Date

_____   _____
Personnel Manager   Date

NOTICE OF PROBATION

Date:

To:

You have received earlier warnings of unsatisfactory performance or violation of our personnel rules.

As you can understand, we do everything possible to retain good employees. When repeated violations or poor performance continues, we usually have no other choice but to dismiss the employee.

However, we do want to give you one final opportunity to prove your value to our company. With that objective we are placing you on a   -month probation. If there is continued unsatisfactory performance during this probationary period, we shall have no alternative but to terminate your employment.

Please accept this as a chance to prove to both yourself and us that our confidence in you was justified.

Please contact   upon receipt of this notice, as we do want to review your employment record with you, clarify the conditions of probation and assist you in whatever way possible toward improved performance.

Very truly,

_____

Copies to:

FORM N503

NOTICE OF EXTENDED PROBATION

Date:

To:

We refer to our notice of probation dated   , 19   .

We have seen an improvement in your job performance during this probationary period. However, we believe it would be in the best interests of both yourself and the company to extend the probationary period so we may better monitor your job performance and make appropriate recommendations on your future employment.

We therefore extend your probation for a period of   month(s), from   to   , and hope you understand our reason for this action.

Once again, we want to continue to work closely with you during this probationary period and help you to further improve your performance and develop as a valued employee. Please contact me so we may schedule a meeting to review your progress.

Very truly,

_____

EXCESSIVE ABSENTEEISM WARNING

Date:

To:

Dear   :

In accordance with company policy, this letter is to serve as a written warning for your excessive absences. You must immediately improve your attendance record to acceptable standards or further discipline, including termination, may result.

On several occasions I have spoken to you about your poor attendance record, and improvement would be noticed for a time. However, your excessive absences always resumed. For the period covering   through   , you were absent   days, excluding vacations and normal holidays. These absences are detailed below:

Reason: Days:

Any unauthorized future absences may result in termination.

Sincerely,

_____

FORM E503

FIRST WARNING NOTICE

Employee: _____ Employee No.:_____

Shift: _____ Date of warning: _____

Date of violation: _____ Time of violation: _____

Violation

____ Intoxication or drugs   ____ Substandard work   ____ Disobedience

____ Clocking out ahead of time   ____ Wrongful conduct   ____ Tardiness

____ Clocking out wrong time card   ____ Carelessness   ____ Absenteeism

____ Other: _____

Action Taken: _____

_____

_____

Additional Remarks:_____

_____

_____

Employee Comments: _____

_____

_____

     This is your first warning of a company rules violation or unsatisfactory performance. Future violations may lead to immediate dismissal without further notice.

_____
Employee

_____
Supervisor

_____
Personnel Manager

SECOND WARNING NOTICE

Employee: _____ Employee No.:_____

Shift: _____ Date of warning: _____

Date of violation: _____ Time of violation: _____

Violation

____ Intoxication or drugs   ____ Substandard work   ____ Disobedience

____ Clocking out ahead of time   ____ Wrongful conduct   ____ Tardiness

____ Clocking out wrong time card   ____ Carelessness   ____ Absenteeism

____ Other: _____

Action Taken:_____

_____

_____

Additional Remarks:_____

_____

_____

Employee Comments: _____

_____

_____

    This is your second warning of a company rules violation or unsatisfactory performance. Future violations may lead to immediate dismissal without further notice.

_____
Employee

_____
Supervisor

_____
Personnel Manager

FORM S501

DISCIPLINARY NOTICE

Employee:_____ Department: _____

Written Warning (   )   Final Warning (   )

1.   Statement of the problem: (violation of rules, policies, standards or practices, or unsatisfactory performance)

2.   Prior, if any, discussion or warnings on this subject, whether oral or written. (List Dates):

3.   Company policy on this subject:

4.   Summary of corrective action to be taken by the company and/or employee:

5.   Consequences of failure to improve performance or correct behavior:

6.   Employee statement: (continue on reverse, if necessary)

_____   _____
Employee   Date

_____   _____
Supervisor   Date

FORM D501   **- 202 -**

DISCIPLINARY WARNING

Employee: _____ Department: _____

Position: _____

Date of Incident: _____ Incident: _____

Reason for Notice: _____

_____

Action taken on this notice:

_____ First warning - Verbal

_____ Second warning - Written

_____ Suspension for   days

_____ Other (specify): _____

_____

Next step for repeated infraction:

_____ Second warning - Written

_____ Suspension for   days

_____ Other (specify): _____

_____

Supervisor Comments: _____

_____

Employee Comments: _____

_____

_____   _____
Supervisor   Date

_____   _____
Employee   Date

FORM D502

DISCIPLINARY REPORT

Employee: _____ Date: _____

Department: _____

Nature of offense: _____

Date of offense: _____ Time: _____

Location of offense: _____

Reported by: _____ Title: _____

Department: _____

Witnesses: _____

Comments: _____

_____

_____

_____

_____

_____   _____
Supervisor   Date

_____   _____
Employee   Date

Offense Number: _____ Date of last offense: _____

Past action taken: _____

Recommendations: _____

_____

The above offense(s) has been documented and made a part of the above employee's
personnel file.

_____   _____
Personnel department   Date

SUSPENSION WITHOUT PAY NOTICE

Date:

To:

Dear   :

    This letter is to inform you that you are hereby suspended from your job for
working days commencing   .
This disciplinary action is being taken based on the following facts:

    Your conduct as described above constitutes sufficient cause for disciplinary action.
In addition, you have been disciplined previously for the same problem.

    Your formal disciplinary action is:

    A copy of this letter will be placed in your personnel file. You have the right to
respond in writing to present information or arguments rebutting this suspension. If you
choose to respond, you have until 5 p.m.
to do so. Your response, if any, will be considered prior to the imposition of the proposed
suspension. It will be assumed that you have waived the right to respond if you do not
take advantage of the above alternative.

    The purpose of this suspension is to impress upon you the seriousness with which
we regard the above violation of employment conditions and to give you the opportunity
to reflect upon your future compliance with our employment standards. If you continue to
violate the conditions of your employment, you may be terminated.

Sincerely,

_____

FORM S502

EMPLOYEE SELF-EVALUATION

CONFIDENTIAL

Employee: _____ Date: _____

My most successful job accomplishments since last performance period are:

1. _____

2. _____

3. _____

4. _____

My least successful job accomplishments since last performance period are:

1. _____

2. _____

3. _____

My key strengths are:

1. _____

2. _____

3. _____

My weakest areas are:

1. _____

2. _____

Action I will take to improve performance: _____

_____

_____

_____

PERFORMANCE ANALYSIS EMPLOYEE WORKSHEET

To (Employee): _____

    To prepare for your upcoming performance review on   ,
I would like you to think about the questions that follow, so we can fully utilize the time
we have for discussion during your review.

1.   How successful overall were you in meeting your performance objectives for this
appraisal period?

2.   Do you feel your performance objectives are appropriate for your job?

3.   Are there areas of concern in your job that you would like to discuss?

4.   What strengths do you have that enhance your performance on the job?

5.   What weaknesses do you have that diminish your performance?

6.   What additional training do you feel you need in order to do a better job?

7.   In what ways can we help you do your job better? Do you feel my supervisory style
enables you to or prohibits you from reaching your potential? Why?

8.   What are your short-term employment goals? How do you feel you can best achieve
these goals?

9.   What are your long-range employment goals? How do you feel you can best achieve
these goals?

10.   What else concerning your job would you like to discuss?

EMPLOYEE PERFORMANCE CHECKLIST

Employee: _____ Date: _____

Department: _____ Period from:_____ to _____

Supervisor: _____

	Excellent	Good	Fair	Poor
Honesty:	_____	_____	_____	_____
Productivity:	_____	_____	_____	_____
Work Quality:	_____	_____	_____	_____
Work Consistency:	_____	_____	_____	_____
Skills:	_____	_____	_____	_____
Enthusiasm:	_____	_____	_____	_____
Attitude:	_____	_____	_____	_____
Cooperation:	_____	_____	_____	_____
Initiative:	_____	_____	_____	_____
Working Relations:	_____	_____	_____	_____
Attendance:	_____	_____	_____	_____
Punctuality:	_____	_____	_____	_____
Dependability:	_____	_____	_____	_____
Appearance:	_____	_____	_____	_____

Other: _____   _____   _____   _____   _____

_____   _____   _____   _____   _____

Comments: _____

_____

_____

_____   _____

Supervisor   Date

NEW EMPLOYEE EVALUATION

Employee: _____ Date: _____

Employment Date: _____ Department: _____

Probation Period: _____ Supervisor: _____

	Excellent	Good	Fair	Poor
Quality of Work:	_____	_____	_____	_____
Quantity of Work:	_____	_____	_____	_____
Knowledge of Job:	_____	_____	_____	_____
Dependability:	_____	_____	_____	_____
Working Relations:	_____	_____	_____	_____
Attitude:	_____	_____	_____	_____
Cooperation:	_____	_____	_____	_____
Potential:	_____	_____	_____	_____

1. This employee should be: Retained (   )   Promoted (   )   Terminated (   )

Why?

2. What are employee's weaknesses/deficiencies? What steps should be taken to correct deficiencies?

3. What strengths does this employee have? How can they best be used by company?

FORM N505

4. What are this employee's long-term employment prospects?

5. Is the employee dissatisfied with the company? The position? What steps should be taken to improve working/job conditions?

6. Other comments on employee's performance, work, record, potential, etc.

_____
Supervisor

MANAGERIAL EVALUATION

Name:_____ Date: _____

Position/Title:_____ Supervisor: _____

PART I. Performance Assessment

Objectives:_____

_____

_____

_____

_____

_____

_____

Rating: Outstanding(   )   Excellent(   )   Good(   )   Fair(   )   Unsatisfactory(   )

PART II: Current Potential Assessment

_____ Promotable

_____ Promotable with additional experience/training

_____ Limited or no potential

Reasons for Above Evaluation: _____

_____

_____

_____

Employee Career Goals: _____

_____

_____

_____

FORM M501

PART III: Developmental Plans

Major areas requiring performance improvement: _____

_____

_____

_____

_____

Action plan for improvement: _____

_____

_____

_____

_____

Completion Date: _____

Other Comments: _____

_____

_____

_____

_____   _____
Signed/Title   Date

_____   _____
Signed/Title   Date

Evaluation discussed with employee on (date): _____

PERFORMANCE EVALUATION

Employee: _____ Position: _____

Department: _____ From: _____ to _____

	Excellent	Good	Fair	Poor
Job Knowledge:	_____	_____	_____	_____
Relations:	_____	_____	_____	_____
Work Quality:	_____	_____	_____	_____
Responsibility:	_____	_____	_____	_____
Quantity of work:	_____	_____	_____	_____
Enthusiasm:	_____	_____	_____	_____
Attitude:	_____	_____	_____	_____
Initiative:	_____	_____	_____	_____
Attendance:	_____	_____	_____	_____
Appearance:	_____	_____	_____	_____
Dependability:	_____	_____	_____	_____
Overall rating:	_____	_____	_____	_____

For Probationary Rating Only:

Recommended for: Permanent Employment (   )   Dismissal (   )

_____
Signed

FORM P502

PRODUCTION PERSONNEL EVALUATION

Employee: _____ Date: _____

Started Work: _____ Review Date: _____

Department: _____ Supervisor: _____

General Performance:	Excellent	Good	Fair	Poor
Attitude:	_____	_____	_____	_____
Skills:	_____	_____	_____	_____
Punctuality:	_____	_____	_____	_____
Dependability:	_____	_____	_____	_____
Initiative:	_____	_____	_____	_____
Cooperation:	_____	_____	_____	_____
Productivity:	_____	_____	_____	_____
Work Quality:	_____	_____	_____	_____

Comments: _____

_____

_____

_____

_____

_____

_____

Comparison to Last Rating:_____

_____

_____

_____

Supervisor

SALES PERSONNEL EVALUATION

Employee: _____   Date: _____

Territory: _____

Period from: _____ to _____

Sales Performance:

Net Sales _____

Sales Quota _____

Above/Below Quota By _____%

Sales Activity:

Sales Calls/Week _____

Sales Reports:

Quality of Reports _____

Timeliness of Reports _____

Other Comments: _____

_____

_____

_____

_____

_____
Signed/Title

FORM S503

STANDARD EVALUATION

Employee: _____ Date: _____

Department:_____ Supervisor:_____

Period from: _____ to_____

Knowledge of Job:_____

_____

_____

_____

_____

Quality of Work: _____

_____

_____

_____

_____

Productivity: _____

_____

_____

_____

_____

Dependability: _____

_____

_____

_____

_____

Cooperation:_____

_____

_____

_____

_____

Attitude:_____

_____

_____

_____

_____

Punctuality:_____

_____

_____

_____

_____

Overall Rating:_____

_____

_____

_____

_____

_____
Supervisor/Reviewer

_____
Employee

FORM S504 *Continiued*

TEMPORARY EMPLOYEE EVALUATION

Employee: _____ Date Hired: _____

Position: _____

Department: _____ Supervisor: _____

	Excellent	Good	Fair	Poor
Work Quality:	_____	_____	_____	_____
Work Quantity:	_____	_____	_____	_____
Cooperation:	_____	_____	_____	_____
Adaptability:	_____	_____	_____	_____
Initiative:	_____	_____	_____	_____
Dependability:	_____	_____	_____	_____
Appearance:	_____	_____	_____	_____
Attendance:	_____	_____	_____	_____
Punctuality:	_____	_____	_____	_____
Growth Potential:	_____	_____	_____	_____

Recommendations

_____ Permanent hiring as _____ at salary of $_____.

_____ Termination.

_____ Continuation on probationary or temporary status.

_____   _____
Evaluator   Date

EMPLOYEE PERFORMANCE REVIEW

Employee: _____ Date: _____

Position: _____ Date Hired: _____

Department: _____ Supervisor: _____

Appraisal Period From: _____ to _____

Merit (   )   Transfer (   )   Promotion (   )   Other (   ) _____

List employee's strengths.

_____

_____

_____

_____

_____

Provide specific examples of employee's major achievements during the review period.

_____

_____

_____

_____

_____

How can employee improve performance?

_____

_____

_____

_____

_____

PERFORMANCE APPRAISAL INTERVIEW REPORT

Employee: _____ Date: _____

Department: _____

Reviewed By: _____ Review Period: _____

Objective: _____

Performance Standard: _____

Results: _____

Remarks: _____

Objective: _____

Performance Standard: _____

Results: _____

Remarks: _____

Objective: _____

Performance Standard: _____

Results: _____

Remarks: _____

Supervisor's recommendations: _____

_____

_____

_____   _____
Supervisor   Date

_____   _____
Employee   Date

EMPLOYEE RATING RESPONSE

Employee:_____

Performance Evaluation Dated: _____

1. I have discussed with my supervisor the evaluation of my past performance.
    I ____ agree ____ do not agree with ____all ____some of the conclusions reached,
    because:

2. I feel that my performance review ____was ____was not fair and impartial, because:

3. If I could make changes or improvements in my work or company policies, I would
    suggest:

_____   _____
Supervisor   Date

_____   _____
Employee   Date

_____   _____
Evaluator   Date

FORM E507

PERFORMANCE OBJECTIVES

Employee: _____ Date: _____

Performance Objectives

1._____

_____

2._____

_____

3._____

_____

4._____

_____

5._____

_____

6._____

_____

Presented to and reviewed with employee.

_____   _____
Employee   Date

_____   _____
Supervisor   Date

COACHING FORM

Employee: _____ Date: _____

Department: _____ Supervisor: _____

Reason: _____

Comments:

Weak points are   Strong points are

_____   _____

_____   _____

_____   _____

_____   _____

These weaknesses can be   These strengths can be used more
strengthened by: effectively by:

_____   _____

_____   _____

_____   _____

_____   _____

_____   _____

_____   _____

_____   _____

_____   _____

_____   _____
Supervisor   Title

A copy of this report has been given to me and has been discussed with me.

_____   _____
Employee   Date

FORM C502

EMPLOYEE PERFORMANCE IMPROVEMENT PLAN

Employee: _____ Position: _____

Department:_____ Supervisor:_____

Performance Review Date: _____

Overall Performance Rating:_____

Areas of deficiency:_____

_____

_____

Reasons contributing to poor performance: _____

_____

_____

Corrective action to be taken by employee: _____

_____

_____

Assistance provided by supervisor:_____

_____

_____

Next performance review scheduled: _____

Comments: _____

_____

_____

_____

_____

_____   _____
Employee   Date

_____   _____
Supervisor   Date

LETTER OF COMMENDATION

Date:

To:

On behalf of our company, I am very pleased to commend you on your excellent job performance during this last review period from   to   .

Your efforts on behalf of the company are truly appreciated. Only through the devoted and tireless contributions of valued employees like yourself can we confidently look to the future.

Again, on behalf of the company and your co-employees, we salute you for a job well done.

Very truly,

_____

Copies to: Department/Personnel File

FORM L501

SALARY CHANGE REQUEST

Employee:_____ Date Started: _____

Department: _____ Supervisor: _____

Position(s): _____

Last Two Increases

(1) From $_____ to $_____   Date _____

(2) From $_____ to $_____   Date _____

Last Performance Analysis: _____

(   ) **Salary increase recommended**

From $_____ to $_____   Effective _____

_____ Merit   _____ In Budget   _____ Exempt

_____ Adjustment   _____ Not in Budget   _____ Non-Exempt

_____ Promotion (If promotion, attach new job description.)

Reason for increase: _____

_____

(   ) **No salary increase recommended**

Based on performance analysis dated: _____

Other: _____

_____

Comments: _____

_____

_____

_____

_____   _____

Signed   Date

Section 6
Benefits

Form A601   **Accrued Benefits Statement** – Lists type and amount of benefits accrued by specific employee.

Form E601   **Employee Benefits Analysis** – Adds company and employee contribution to a given benefit to determine the total annual cost of the benefit.

Form B601   **Benefits Planning Checklist** – Compares current company benefits with competitor's policy and employee's preferences, and makes a recommendation.

Form E602   **Employee Benefits Survey** – Seeks employees' opinions of current company benefits.

Form E603   **Employee Benefits List** – Outlines benefits offered employees.

Form C601   **Combined Resolution - Incentive Stock Option Plan** – Resolution to adopt incentive stock option plan.

Form R601   **Resolution - Signing Bonus** – Resolution to adopt a signing bonus to induce applicants to accept employment.

Form R602   **Resolution - Paid-Up Annuity Plan** – Resolution to adopt a paid-up annuity plan for a specific employee.

Form R603   **Resolution - Relocation Allowance** – Resolution to reimburse an employee for relocation expenses.

Form R604   **Resolution - Performance Bonus** – Resolution to pay a specific employee a performance bonus.

Form R605   **Resolution - Low-Interest Loan** – Resolution to provide a specific employee with a low-interest loan.

Form R606	**Resolution - Company Car** – Resolution to provide a specific employee with a company car.
Form R607	**Resolution - Club Membership** – Resolution to provide a company club membership.
Form R608	**Resolution - At-Home Entertainment Allowance** – Resolution to reimburse specific employee for at-home entertainment expenses.
Form R609	**Resolution - Tuition Benefit** – Resolution to provide specific employee with tuition.
Form R610	**Resolution - Scholarship Aid Program** – Resolution to provide a scholarship aid program to children of employees.
Form R611	**Resolution - Financial Counseling Plan** – Resolution to provide key employees with financial counseling plan.
Form R612	**Resolution - Sabbatical Leave** – Resolution to provide specific employee a sabbatical leave for a specific purpose.
Form R613	**Resolution - Child Care Plan** – Resolution to provide child care program for children of employees.
Form R614	**Resolution - Wage Continuation Plan** – Resolution to continue wages for sick and injured employees.
Form R615	**Resolution - Merchandise Discount Program** – Resolution to provide employees with discounted merchandise.

ACCRUED BENEFITS STATEMENT

Employee: _____

Department: _____ Benefits accrued to (date): _____

Accrued Vacation Days: _____

Accrued Vacation Pay: $_____

Accrued Sick Days: _____

Accrued Sick Pay: $_____

Cash Value Life Insurance: $_____

Non-Vested Profit-Sharing: $_____

Vested Profit-Sharing: $_____

Stock Dividends: $_____

Company Shares: _____

Vested Pension: $_____

Non-Vested Pension: $_____

Credit Union Balance: $_____

Severance Pay: $_____

Accrued Reimbursable Expenses: $_____

Other Benefits:

_____   _____

_____   _____

_____   _____

This is an _____ interim _____ final statement.

This statement is subject to corrections.

_____   _____
Signed   Date

EMPLOYEE BENEFITS ANALYSIS

	Company Contribution	Employee Contribution	Benefit Total Cost (Annual)
Retirement Plan:	$ _____	$ _____	$ _____
Deferred Compensation:	$ _____	$ _____	$ _____
Incentive Stock Option:	$ _____	$ _____	$ _____
Disability Insurance:	$ _____	$ _____	$ _____
Health Insurance:	$ _____	$ _____	$ _____
Group Life Insurance:	$ _____	$ _____	$ _____
Dental Insurance:	$ _____	$ _____	$ _____
Education Benefits:	$ _____	$ _____	$ _____
Profit-Sharing:	$ _____	$ _____	$ _____
Performance Bonus:	$ _____	$ _____	$ _____
Scholarship Aid:	$ _____	$ _____	$ _____
Relocation Expense:	$ _____	$ _____	$ _____
Group Legal:	$ _____	$ _____	$ _____
Wage Continuation:	$ _____	$ _____	$ _____
Child Care:	$ _____	$ _____	$ _____
Club Memberships:	$ _____	$ _____	$ _____
Stock Purchase Plan:	$ _____	$ _____	$ _____
Paid-Up Annuities:	$ _____	$ _____	$ _____
Low-Interest Loans:	$ _____	$ _____	$ _____
Company Car:	$ _____	$ _____	$ _____
Financial Counseling:	$ _____	$ _____	$ _____
Sabbaticals:	$ _____	$ _____	$ _____
At-Home Entertainment:	$ _____	$ _____	$ _____
Other: _____	$ _____	$ _____	$ _____

BENEFITS PLANNING CHECKLIST

	Company Policy	Competitor Policy	Employee Prefernce	Recommendation
Retirement Plan:	_____	_____	_____	_____
Deferred Compensation:	_____	_____	_____	_____
Incentive Stock Option:	_____	_____	_____	_____
Disability Insurance:	_____	_____	_____	_____
Health Insurance:	_____	_____	_____	_____
Group Life Insurance:	_____	_____	_____	_____
Dental Insurance:	_____	_____	_____	_____
Education Benefits:	_____	_____	_____	_____
Profit-Sharing:	_____	_____	_____	_____
Performance Bonus:	_____	_____	_____	_____
Scholarship Aid:	_____	_____	_____	_____
Relocation Expense:	_____	_____	_____	_____
Group Legal:	_____	_____	_____	_____
Wage Continuation:	_____	_____	_____	_____
Child Care:	_____	_____	_____	_____
Club Memberships:	_____	_____	_____	_____
Stock Purchase Plan:	_____	_____	_____	_____
Paid-Up Annuities:	_____	_____	_____	_____
Low-Interest Loans:	_____	_____	_____	_____
Company Car:	_____	_____	_____	_____
Financial Counseling:	_____	_____	_____	_____
Sabbaticals:	_____	_____	_____	_____
At-Home Entertainment:	_____	_____	_____	_____
Other:	_____	_____	_____	_____

FORM B601

EMPLOYEE BENEFITS SURVEY

We want your opinion on the importance of each employee benefit presently offered, as well as other benefits under consideration. Please rank each benefit listed in order of relative interest to you. Use a 1-10 scale, 1 meaning top priority and 10 indicating the lowest priority items. Your comments are also invited.

Benefit	Priority	Comments
Retirement Plan:	_____	_____
Deferred Compensation:	_____	_____
Incentive Stock Option:	_____	_____
Disability Insurance:	_____	_____
Health Insurance:	_____	_____
Group Life Insurance:	_____	_____
Dental Insurance:	_____	_____
Education Benefit:	_____	_____
Profit-Sharing:	_____	_____
Performance Bonus:	_____	_____
Scholarship Aid:	_____	_____
Relocation Expense:	_____	_____
Group Legal:	_____	_____
Wage Continuation:	_____	_____
Child Care:	_____	_____
Club Memberships:	_____	_____
Stock Purchase Plan:	_____	_____
Paid-Up Annuities:	_____	_____
Low-Interest Loans:	_____	_____
Company Car:	_____	_____
Financial Counseling:	_____	_____
Sabbaticals:	_____	_____
At-Home Entertainment:	_____	_____
Other: _____	_____	_____

EMPLOYEE BENEFITS LIST

Benefit

Description

_____

_____

_____

_____

_____

_____

_____

_____

_____

_____

_____

_____

_____

_____

_____

_____

_____

_____

_____

_____

_____

_____

_____

_____

_____

_____

_____

_____

FORM E603

COMBINED RESOLUTION
INCENTIVE STOCK OPTION PLAN

A special combined meeting of the stockholders and directors of the corporation was duly called and held at   , on   , 19   , at   m.

A necessary quorum of stockholders and directors was present and voting throughout or otherwise consented to this action.

Upon motions duly made, seconded, and carried it was

VOTED to adopt, effective   , 19   , a certain Incentive Stock Option Plan in the form as annexed.

VOTED that the President of the Corporation be authorized to execute all documents and undertake all acts reasonably necessary to accomplish the foregoing.

VOTED to adjourn.

I hereby certify the foregoing is a true record of said meeting.

A TRUE RECORD

ATTEST

_____
Secretary

RESOLUTION
SIGNING BONUS

A special meeting of the Board of Directors was duly called and held at
_____ , on _____ , 19 _____ , at _____ m.

All the directors waived notice of and were present at or consented to the actions taken at the meeting.

Upon motions duly made, seconded, and carried it was

VOTED to pay to _____ a signing bonus in the amount of $ _____ , which bonus shall be an inducement for accepting employment with the Corporation.

VOTED that the President of the Corporation, or such designee as may be appointed, be further authorized to execute such documents and undertake such acts as are reasonably incidental or necessary to accomplish the foregoing.

VOTED to adjourn, there being no further business to transact.

I hereby certify the foregoing is a true record of said meeting.

A TRUE RECORD

ATTEST

_____
Secretary

RESOLUTION
PAID-UP ANNUITY PLAN

A special meeting of the Board of Directors was duly called and held at
                              , on   , 19   ,
at   m. All the directors waived notice of and were present at or consented to the
actions taken at the meeting.

Upon motions duly made, seconded, and carried it was

VOTED to adopt, effective   , a paid-up annuity
plan on behalf of   , wherein the Corporation
shall make a series of payments into a designated savings account wherein it is
anticipated that said annuity shall equal $ in   years
from date hereof.

VOTED that the President of the Corporation, or such designee as may be appointed,
be further authorized to execute such documents and undertake such acts as are
reasonably incidental or necessary to accomplish the foregoing.

VOTED to adjourn, there being no further business to transact.

I hereby certify the foregoing is a true record of said meeting.

A TRUE RECORD

ATTEST

_____
Secretary

RESOLUTION
RELOCATION ALLOWANCE

A special meeting of the Board of Directors was duly called and held at
_____ , on _____ ,19____ , at ____ m.

All the directors waived notice of and were present at or consented to the actions taken at the meeting.

Upon motions duly made, seconded, and carried it was

VOTED that the Corporation reimburse _____ , as a relocation allowance, the sum of $_____ .

VOTED that the President of the Corporation, or such designee as may be appointed, be further authorized to execute such documents and undertake such acts as are reasonably incidental or necessary to accomplish the foregoing.

VOTED to adjourn, there being no further business to transact.

I hereby certify the foregoing is a true record of said meeting.

A TRUE RECORD

ATTEST

_____
Secretary

FORM R603

RESOLUTION
PERFORMANCE BONUS

A special meeting of the Board of Directors was duly called and held at
_____ , on _____ , 19___ , at ___ m.

All the directors waived notice of and were present at or consented to the actions taken at the meeting.

Upon motions duly made, seconded, and carried it was

VOTED to pay to _____ a performance bonus in the amount of $_____ in recognition of the accomplishments of said employee(s) during the prior _____ .

VOTED that the President of the Corporation, or such designee as may be appointed, be further authorized to execute such documents and undertake such acts as are reasonably incidental or necessary to accomplish the foregoing.

VOTED to adjourn, there being no further business to transact.

I hereby certify the foregoing is a true record of said meeting.

A TRUE RECORD

ATTEST

_____
Secretary

RESOLUTION
LOW-INTEREST LOAN

A special meeting of the Board of Directors was duly called and held at
_____ , on _____ , 19_____ , at _____ m.

All the directors waived notice of and were present at or consented to the actions taken at the meeting.

Upon motions duly made, seconded, and carried it was

VOTED to provide _____ a low-interest loan on the following terms:

1. Amount $

2. Annual Interest: %

3. Terms of Repayment:

4. Permitted Use of Proceeds:

5. Loan Security:

VOTED that the President of the Corporation, or such designee as may be appointed, be further authorized to execute such documents and undertake such acts as are reasonably incidental or necessary to accomplish the foregoing.

VOTED to adjourn, there being no further business to transact.

I hereby certify the foregoing is a true record of said meeting.

A TRUE RECORD

ATTEST

_____
Secretary

RESOLUTION
COMPANY CAR

A special meeting of the Board of Directors was duly called and held at
_____, on _____ ,19___ , at ___ m.

All the directors waived notice of and were present at or consented to the actions taken at the meeting.

Upon motions duly made, seconded, and carried it was

VOTED to provide _____ full use of a company car together with all maintenance, insurance, taxes and costs associated with its upkeep, all due to the necessity that said employee has an automobile in fulfillment of employee's duties; provided however, that employee shall apportion and reimburse the Corporation such costs associated with use of said vehicle for personal use.

VOTED that the President of the Corporation, or such designee as may be appointed, be further authorized to execute such documents and undertake such acts as are reasonably incidental or necessary to accomplish the foregoing.

VOTED to adjourn, there being no further business to transact

I hereby certify the foregoing is a true record of said meeting.

A TRUE RECORD

ATTEST

_____
Secretary

RESOLUTION
CLUB MEMBERSHIP

A special meeting of the Board of Directors was duly called and held at
                   , on   ,19   , at   m.

All the directors waived notice of and were present at or consented to the actions taken at the meeting.

Upon motions duly made, seconded, and carried it was

VOTED to provide   a fully paid club membership in   for a period of   year(s) from date hereof; all in recognition that said club membership is desirable and beneficial to the Corporation in that it would provide a place for entertaining customers and suppliers, thereby increasing the corporation's business, and further, the Corporation shall pay or reimburse said employee for all reasonable expenses incurred in connection with business-related entertainment at said club.

VOTED that the President of the Corporation, or such designee as may be appointed, be further authorized to execute such documents and undertake such acts as are reasonably incidental or necessary to accomplish the foregoing.

VOTED to adjourn, there being no further business to transact.

I hereby certify the foregoing is a true record of said meeting.

A TRUE RECORD

ATTEST

_____
Secretary

RESOLUTION
AT-HOME ENTERTAINMENT ALLOWANCE

A special meeting of the Board of Directors was duly called and held at   , on   , 19   , at   m.

All the directors waived notice of and were present at or consented to the actions taken at the meeting.

Upon motions duly made, seconded, and carried it was

VOTED to reimburse   , as an at-home entertainment allowance, such expense vouchers as may from time to time be submitted as incurred in connection with the home entertainment of customers, suppliers and other business associates.

VOTED that the President of the Corporation, or such designee as may be appointed, be further authorized to execute such documents and undertake such acts as are reasonably incidental or necessary to accomplish the foregoing.

VOTED to adjourn, there being no further business to transact.

I hereby certify the foregoing is a true record of said meeting.

A TRUE RECORD

ATTEST

_____
Secretary

RESOLUTION
TUITION BENEFIT

A special meeting of the Board of Directors was duly called and held at
                        , on   , 19   , at   m.

All the directors waived notice of and were present at or consented to the actions taken at the meeting.

Upon motions duly made, seconded, and carried it was

VOTED to pay on behalf of   ,
as a tuition benefit, an amount equal to   % of the total tuition (including all directly associated costs) for attendance at the   program at
              ; all in recognition that said program is reasonably necessary to improve the employee's job performance, competence and skills and therefore benefit the Corporation.

VOTED that the President of the Corporation, or such designee as may be appointed, be further authorized to execute such documents and undertake such acts as are reasonably incidental or necessary to accomplish the foregoing.

VOTED to adjourn, there being no further business to transact.

I hereby certify the foregoing is a true record of said meeting.

A TRUE RECORD

ATTEST

_____
Secretary

FORM R609

RESOLUTION
SCHOLARSHIP AID PROGRAM

A special meeting of the Board of Directors was duly called and held at _____, on _____, 19___, at ___ m.

All the directors waived notice of and were present at or consented to the actions taken at the meeting.

Upon motions duly made, seconded, and carried it was

VOTED to provide a scholarship aid program to children of the Corporation employees, and to contribute in this way toward the educational expenses of employees by adopting the scholarship aid program as annexed hereto.

VOTED that the President of the Corporation, or such designee as may be appointed, be further authorized to execute such documents and undertake such acts as are reasonably incidental or necessary to accomplish the foregoing.

VOTED to adjourn, there being no further business to transact.

I hereby certify the foregoing is a true record of said meeting.

A TRUE RECORD

ATTEST

_____
Secretary

RESOLUTION
FINANCIAL COUNSELING PLAN

A special meeting of the Board of Directors was duly called and held at _____, on _____ , 19____ , at ____ m.

All the directors waived notice of and were present at or consented to the actions taken at the meeting.

Upon motions duly made, seconded, and carried it was

VOTED to provide all officers of the Corporation and such key employees as may be designated from time to time a fully paid financial counseling plan providing said employees access to professional financial counseling and wherein said plan is desirable to promote better employer-employee relations.

VOTED that the President of the Corporation, or such designee as may be appointed, be further authorized to execute such documents and undertake such acts as are reasonably incidental or necessary to accomplish the foregoing.

VOTED to adjourn, there being no further business to transact.

I hereby certify the foregoing is a true record of said meeting.

A TRUE RECORD

ATTEST

_____
Secretary

FORM R611

RESOLUTION
SABBATICAL LEAVE

A special meeting of the Board of Directors was duly called and held at
, on , 19 , at m.

All the directors waived notice of and were present at or consented to the actions taken at the meeting.

Upon motions duly made, seconded, and carried it was

VOTED to provide
a sabbatical leave for a period of for purposes of
, during which said employee shall have full continuation of all salaries and benefits.

VOTED that the President of the Corporation, or such designee as may be appointed, be further authorized to execute such documents and undertake such acts as are reasonably incidental or necessary to accomplish the foregoing.

VOTED to adjourn, there being no further business to transact

I hereby certify the foregoing is a true record of said meeting.

A TRUE RECORD

ATTEST

_____
Secretary

RESOLUTION
CHILD CARE PLAN

A special meeting of the Board of Directors was duly called and held at
_____, on _____, 19___, at ___ m.

All the directors waived notice of and were present at or consented to the actions taken at the meeting.

Upon motions duly made, seconded, and carried it was

VOTED to provide employees of the Corporation a Child Care Plan in the form and coverage as annexed, all in recognition that providing adequate day care assistance will improve attendance and be beneficial to the Corporation.

VOTED that the President of the Corporation, or such designee as may be appointed, be further authorized to execute such documents and undertake such acts as are reasonably incidental or necessary to accomplish the foregoing.

VOTED to adjourn, there being no further business to transact.

I hereby certify the foregoing is a true record of said meeting.

A TRUE RECORD

ATTEST

_____
Secretary

FORM R613

RESOLUTION
WAGE CONTINUATION PLAN

A special meeting of the Board of Directors was duly called and held at
             , on   , 19   , at   m.

All the directors waived notice of and were present at or consented to the actions taken at the meeting.

Upon motions duly made, seconded, and carried it was

VOTED to adopt a Wage Continuation Plan on behalf of sick and injured employees, said plan being non-funded by insurance, but deemed to be in addition to any disability insurance or workmen's compensation benefits payable; and wherein said plan is on the terms annexed.

VOTED that the President of the Corporation, or such designee as may be appointed, be further authorized to execute such documents and undertake such acts as are reasonably incidental or necessary to accomplish the foregoing.

VOTED to adjourn, there being no further business to transact.

I hereby certify the foregoing is a true record of said meeting.

A TRUE RECORD

ATTEST

_____
Secretary

RESOLUTION
MERCHANDISE DISCOUNT PROGRAM

A special meeting of the Board of Directors was duly called and held at
                          , on   , 19   , at   m.

All the directors waived notice of and were present at or consented to the actions taken at the meeting.

Upon motions duly made, seconded, and carried it was

VOTED to adopt, effective   , a Merchandise Discount Program in the form as annexed and as may from time to time be modified by management of the Corporation.

VOTED that the President of the Corporation, or such designee as may be appointed, be further authorized to execute such documents and undertake such acts as are reasonably incidental or necessary to accomplish the foregoing.

VOTED to adjourn, there being no further business to transact.

I hereby certify the foregoing is a true record of said meeting.

A TRUE RECORD

TEST

_____
Secretary

FORM R615

Section 7
Termination/Separation

Form R701	**Retirement Checklist** – Lists information required for retirement.
Form R702	**Resignation** – Employee's letter of resignation.
Form T701	**Termination Checklist** – Lists information to be completed upon termination.
Form N701	**Notice of Dismissal** – Notifies employee of termination.
Form N702	**Notice of Termination Due to Absence** – Notifies employee of termination because of excess absenteeism.
Form N703	**Notice of Termination Due to Work Rules Violation** – Notifies employee of termination because of a violation of work rules.
Form R703	**Reduction in Workforce Notice** – Notifies employee of termination because of a reduction in the company's workforce.
Form T702	**Termination Letter for Excessive Absenteeism** – Notifies employee of termination because of excessive absenteeism.
Form T703	**Termination Letter for Lack of Work** – Notifies employee of termination because of lack of work.
Form T704	**Termination Letter for Intoxication on the Job** – Notifies employee of termination because of intoxication on the job.
Form L701	**Letter Terminating Sales Representative** – Notifies sales representative of termination.
Form E701	**Employee Checkout Record** – Provides record of items to be returned and completed by terminated employee.
Form G701	**General Release** – Releases employee and company from any liability resulting from employee's employment with company.

Form M701	**Mutual Release** – Mutually releases employee and company from any liability resulting from employee's employment with company.
Form E702	**Employee Release** – Releases company from any claims of liability from employee.
Form E703	**Employee Exit Interview** – Employee questionnaire regarding termination.
Form S701	**Separation Notice** – Records events of employee's separation from company.
Form P701	**Personnel Separation Report** – Records reasons for termination.
Form E704	**Employee Separation Report** – Summarizes evaluation of employee upon termination.
Form U701	**Unemployment Compensation Record** – Records payment of unemployment compensation to a given employee.
Form E705	**EEO Analysis of Terminations** – Analyzes minority makeup of employees terminated.
Form R704	**Reference Report** – Responds to request for reference on a former employee.
Form E706	**Employment Reference Response** – Briefly responds to request for reference on a former employee.
Form R705	**Refusal to Grant References** – Refuses to supply requested information on a former employee.
Form N704	**Notice of Confidentiality Agreement** – Notifies former employee's current employer of employee's confidentiality agreement.
Form C701	**COBRA Letter to Terminating Employee** – Notifies former employee of eligibility of COBRA benefits.
Form C702	**COBRA Employee Information Letter** – Notifies former employee of eligibility of COBRA benefits.
Form C703	**COBRA Compliance** – Record of former employee's COBRA participation.

RETIREMENT CHECKLIST

Employee:_____ Department: _____

1. Letter of Resignation - Submit a Letter of Resignation indicating your upcoming retirement to your supervisor who will forward it to the Human Resources Department. Please include your forwarding address in your letter.

2. Vacation Pay - All vacation earned but not taken prior to retirement will be included in your final pay.

3. Address Change - Your address will be changed automatically when you retire and you will receive your statements at home.

4. Employee Benefits - Contact the Employee Benefits Department for information concerning your continued benefit coverage, as well as accrued benefits.

5. Company Property - If you have been issued any of the following, please arrange to return them to your supervisor:

   _____ Security badge   _____ Supervisor's manual

   _____ ID badge   _____ Keys

   _____ Other _____

FORM R701

RESIGNATION

Date:

To:

     Please be informed that I hereby submit my resignation in all capacities with the company effective:

     Pursuant to company policy and/or the terms of my employment, I shall make appropriate arrangements for the return of company property.

     Any compensation due me or other correspondence may be directed to me at:

     Sincerely,

_____

TERMINATION CHECKLIST

Employee: _____ Date: _____

Department: _____

_____ Voluntary

_____ Involuntary

_____ With Notice

_____ Without Notice

_____ Reason_____

_____

_____ Eligible for rehire?

_____ Vacation pay period?

_____ Transfer to referral status? (will need Referral Agreement)

_____ Resignation/Separation Notice completed

_____ License information

_____ Return of all company property, including keys and parking pass, telephone codes, credit cards, personnel manual.

_____ Paycheck delivered to employee upon termination

_____
Supervisor

_____
Date

NOTICE OF DISMISSAL

Date:

To:

We regret to notify you that your employment with the firm shall be terminated on _____, 19____, for the following reasons:

Severance pay shall be in accordance with company policy. We shall also issue to you a statement of accrued benefits. Insurance benefits shall continue according to applicable law and/or the provisions of our employee policy. Please contact _____ at your earliest convenience, who will arrange other termination matters with you.

We sincerely regret this action is necessary.

Very truly,

_____

Copies to:

NOTICE OF TERMINATION
DUE TO ABSENCE

Date:

To:

We regret to inform you that your employment with the company shall terminate on _____, 19____, due to repeated non-authorized absences.

We previously warned you about unauthorized absences in violation of company policy. However, your record shows repeated absences. A copy of your employment attendance record is available for your review.

Severance pay shall be in accordance with company policy. We shall issue to you a statement of accrued benefits. Insurance benefits shall continue in accordance with applicable law and/or the provisions of our employee policy. Please contact _____ at your earliest convenience, who will arrange other termination matters with you.

We sincerely regret this action is necessary.

Very truly

_____

Copies to:

NOTICE OF TERMINATION
DUE TO WORK RULES VIOLATION

Date:

To:

    You are hereby given notice that your employment with the company shall be terminated on   , 19   .

    This action is necessary due to the following violations of company work rules:

    Your final paycheck shall be for the period ending   . There shall be no severance pay since your termination was for just cause. Please contact   concerning insurance coverage or other accrued benefits to which you may be entitled.

    We regret this action is necessary, and wish you success in your future endeavors.

                   Sincerely,

_____

REDUCTION IN WORKFORCE NOTICE

Date:

To:

Dear   :

Due to current economic conditions, we have found it necessary to reduce employees, and for that reason we are terminating your employment effective   . The company agrees to pay you, however, for an additional 30 days through   ; all unused and accrued vacation; and severance pay at the rate of two weeks for each year of service up to a maximum of 26 weeks.

You understand and agree that this severance payment is in lieu of all other payments and benefits due you as a result of your employment with us except those payments and benefits specifically identified in this letter.

In addition to termination pay, severance pay, and vacation pay, the company will pay your medical insurance coverage through   . All other benefits cease   . You will have the right to continue medical coverage at your own expense for an additional 18 months.

The company is also prepared to provide job search counseling and resume assistance to those employees who request it. Please notify us no later than   if you wish to receive these services.

A letter reviewing specific details of your particular benefits and severance pay will be mailed to your home.

We wish you the best of luck in your future career endeavors.

Sincerely,

_____

TERMINATION LETTER FOR EXCESSIVE ABSENTEEISM

Date:

To:

Dear   :

As stated in my letter to you of   , your record of absence from work has kept you from performing the full schedule of assignments for your position. I further indicated that a continuation of absences could lead to your termination.

A current review of your attendance indicates that since that warning you have been absent from work for   out of the last   days.

In view of your poor attendance record, I am recommending to the Personnel Director, by copy of this letter, that your employment with the company be terminated effective

Should you desire to meet for the purpose of discussing this intended action, please notify us within ten working days after receipt of this letter.

Sincerely,

_____

TERMINATION LETTER FOR LACK OF WORK

Date:

To:

Dear   :

    Please be advised that we are terminating your employment effective
                    . However, in view of your service to the company, we agree to pay
you the following severence:

Regular wages	$	_____
Vacation ( ):	$	_____
Severence Pay	$	_____
Subtotal	$	_____
Less: Federal Withholding	$	_____
FICA	$	_____
Other	$	_____
Net:	$	_____

    You may choose to continue your medical insurance coverage at your expense. You must decide within 60 days of your termination. If you decide to continue coverage, contact   in the benefits office for additional information.

    You understand and agree that this severence payment constitutes all payments and benefits due you as a result of your employment by
and its parent or affiliate companies.

Sincerely,

_____

Read and accepted:

_____   _____
Employee   Date

TERMINATION LETTER FOR INTOXICATION ON THE JOB

Date:

To:

Dear   :

This letter is to inform you that we are terminating your employment effective
. This decision is based on an incident report submitted to me on
by your supervisor,   .
The report recommended your termination because of your intoxication during working hours.

As you are aware, the first reported incident of your intoxication on the job was
. That report was placed in your personnel file, and you were informed at that time that another incident would result in a disciplinary action or possible dismissal.

This second incident of intoxication adversely affected the operational efficiency and effectiveness of your department and threatened the safety of other employees.

Your final paycheck, including all forms of compensation due you, can be picked up in the Personnel Office on your way out. You may continue your medical coverage for a period of 18 months if you notify us within the next 60 days of your intent to do so and send us your check for $ each month to cover your medical premiums.

Sincerely,

_____

Personnel Manager

LETTER TERMINATING SALES REPRESENTATIVE

Date:

To:

     We regret to notify you that your sales representative agreement with the firm shall be terminated on   , 19   , because of the following reasons:

     Severance pay and any outstanding commissions shall be paid in accordance with our agreement. Within 30 days of termination we shall issue to you a statement of accrued benefits. Any insurance benefits shall continue in accordance with applicable law and/or the provisions of our personnel policy. Please contact   , at your earliest convenience, who will explain each of these items and arrange with you for the return of any company property.

     We sincerely regret this action is necessary.

Very truly,

_____

Copies to:

FORM L701

EMPLOYEE CHECKOUT RECORD

Employee:_____ Department: _____

Termination Date: _____

Complete or return each of the below checked items upon termination.

Return	(check)	(check)	Complete	(check)	(check)
ID Badge:	_____	_____	Exit Interview	_____	_____
Company Tools:	_____	_____	Expense Reports	_____	_____
Desk/File Keys:	_____	_____	Terminations Form	_____	_____
Security Statement:	_____	_____	Confidentiality Report	_____	_____
Air Travel Cards:	_____	_____	Other: _____	_____	_____
Credit Cards:	_____	_____	_____	_____	_____
Petty Cash Advances:	_____	_____	_____	_____	_____
Expense Accounts:	_____	_____	_____	_____	_____
Keys to Premises:	_____	_____			
Catalog/Sales Items:	_____	_____			
Sample Products:	_____	_____			
Vehicles:	_____	_____			
Company Documents:	_____	_____			
Customer Lists:	_____	_____			
Other:					
_____	_____	_____			
_____	_____	_____			
_____	_____	_____			

_____   _____
Supervisor   Date

GENERAL RELEASE

For good consideration and in consideration of the mutual promises hereby made, (Employee) and
(Company) do hereby mutually and reciprocally release and discharge one and the other from all contracts, agreements, claims, actions, demands both in law and in equity, rights, benefits, (excepting those benefits that survive by law) and suits of every nature and description arising from the employment relationship previously existing between Company and Employee.

This release shall be binding upon and inure to the benefit of the parties, their successors, assigns, personal representatives, and heirs, and without limiting the generality of the foregoing officers, directors, employees and agents of the Company.

Signed under seal this   day of   , 19   .

_____
Employee

_____
Company
By: _____

FORM G701

MUTUAL RELEASE

BE IT KNOWN, for good consideration, and in further consideration of the mutual releases herein entered into, that:

(Company) and
(Employee) do hereby completely, mutually and reciprocally release, discharge, acquit and forgive each other from all claims, contracts, actions, suits, demands, agreements, liabilities, and proceedings of every nature and description both at law and in equity that either party has or may have against the other, arising from the beginning of time to the date of these presence, including but not necessarily limited to any incident or claim resulting from employment with said Company.

This release shall be binding upon and inure to the benefit of the parties, their successors, assigns and personal representatives.

Signed this   day of   , 19   .

_____
Employee

_____
Company
By: _____

EMPLOYEE RELEASE

IN GOOD CONSIDERATION of employment, the undersigned
(Employee) hereby forever releases,
discharges, acquits and forgives
(Company) from any and all claims, actions, suits, demands, agreements, and each of them, if more than one, liabilities, judgment, and proceedings both at law and in equity arising from the beginning of time to the date of these presents and as more particularly related to or arising from said employment.

This release shall be binding upon and inure to the benefit of the parties, their successors, assigns and personal representatives.

Signed this   day of   , 19   .

_____
Employee

In the presence of: _____
Witness

FORM E702

EMPLOYEE EXIT INTERVIEW

Employee:_____ Position:_____

Department:_____ Supervisor: _____

Employed From: _____ To: _____

Reason For Termination: _____

Employee Returned:

_____ keys   _____ safety equipment   _____ tools

_____ ID card   _____ company documents   _____ uniform

_____ credit card   _____ other company property   _____ company vehicle

Employee was informed about restrictions on:

_____ trade secrets   _____ removing company documents

_____ patents   _____ employment with competitor (if applicable)

_____ other_____

Employee exit questions/answers:

1. Did management adequately recognize your contributions? _____

    _____

2. Did you feel that you had the support of management? _____

    _____

3. Were you properly trained for your job? _____

    _____

4. Was your work rewarding? _____

    _____

5. Were you fairly treated by the company?_____

    _____

6. Was your salary adequate? _____

_____

7. How were your working conditions? _____

_____

8. Were you supervised properly? _____

_____

9. Did you understand all company policies? _____

_____

10. Have you seen theft of company property? _____

_____

11. How can the company improve security? _____

_____

12. How can the company improve working conditions? _____

_____

13. What do you feel are the company's strengths? _____

_____

14. What do you feel are the company's weaknesses? _____

_____

15. Other employee comments or suggestions: _____

_____

SEPARATION NOTICE

Company: _____

Employee: _____

Social Security No.: _____ Job Title: _____

Dates of Employment: Start: _____ Last: _____

Working Hours: _____ to: _____ Days: _____

Rate of Pay: _____ per _____ Paid overtime? Yes ( )   No ( )

Amount of pay given in lieu of notice, if any: _____

Voluntary quit ( )   Discharged ( )   Lack of work ( )   Other ( ) _____

What circumstance led to separation? _____

_____

What other circumstances, if any, were taken into consideration? _____

_____

Employee's comments: _____

_____

_____   _____
Employee   Date

_____   _____
Supervisor/Title   Date

_____   _____
Witness   Date

Would you rehire this individual? Yes ( )   No ( )

Attach supporting documents as applicable (warning notices, application forms, doctor's statements). This form should be completed immediately at separation time.

PERSONNEL SEPARATION REPORT

The following employee was separated on: _____

Employee: _____ Social Security No.:_____

Department: _____ Supervisor: _____

Job Title: _____

Reason for separation:

_____ Layoff   _____ Retirement

_____ Discharge due to performance   _____ Resignation

_____ Discharge, disciplinary   _____ Resignation requested

Comments: _____

_____

_____

_____

Compensation paid after separation:

    Vacation pay: _____ Yes _____ No

    Severance pay: _____ Yes _____ No

Report issued by: _____ Title:_____

Date:_____

FORM P701

EMPLOYEE SEPARATION REPORT

Employee: _____ Date: _____

Department: _____ Supervisor: _____

Position: _____

Termination Date: _____ Pay Through: _____

Reason for Termination: _____

_____

Unemployment Compensation Eligibility: _____

Severance Pay Eligibility: _____

_____

Continued Benefits Eligibility: _____

_____

_____

Overall Evaluation of Employee: _____

_____

_____

Should Employee be Rehired if Position Open? _____

_____

_____

Comments: _____

_____

_____

_____   _____
Supervisor   Date

Use reverse side for additional comments if necessary

UNEMPLOYMENT COMPENSATION RECORD

Employee:_____ Social Security No.: _____

Department: _____ Position:_____

Date Hired: _____ Date Terminated:_____

Reason for Termination: _____

_____

Unemployment Compensation Charged to Company:

$ _____ weekly for _____weeks

Was the claim accepted? _____ Yes _____ No

If no, date and number of review board appeal: _____

_____

Review Board Findings : _____

_____

Week Ending:_____ Unemployment Comp. Paid _____

Week Ending:_____ Unemployment Comp. Paid _____

Week Ending:_____ Unemployment Comp. Paid _____

Submitted By _____ Date_____

FORM U701

EEO ANALYSIS OF TERMINATIONS

	Male	Minorities	Female	Total Employees	% Minority	% Female
Job Group						
Senior Management:	_____	_____	_____	_____	_____	_____
Middle Management:	_____	_____	_____	_____	_____	_____
Supervisors:	_____	_____	_____	_____	_____	_____
Professionals:	_____	_____	_____	_____	_____	_____
Technicians:	_____	_____	_____	_____	_____	_____
Sales Personnel:	_____	_____	_____	_____	_____	_____
Clerical Personnel:	_____	_____	_____	_____	_____	_____
Service Personnel:	_____	_____	_____	_____	_____	_____
Total:	_____	_____	_____	_____	_____	_____

REFERENCE REPORT

Date:

To:

Re:

In reply to your request for a reference on the above-named former employee, I provide the following information:

1. Position held: _____

2. Dates employed: _____ to _____

3. Salary on termination: _____

4. Reason for termination:_____

_____

_____

5. Overall performance:_____

_____

_____

6. Other comments: _____

_____

_____

7. We would_____ would not_____ rehire.

We request that you keep this reference confidential.

Sincerely,

_____

Personnel Manager

FORM R704

EMPLOYMENT REFERENCE RESPONSE

Employee:_____

Dates of service: From _____ to _____

Position at termination: _____

Reason for termination: _____

Note: This company has a policy of issuing brief, standardized reports in response to all employment reference requests. This report is used for all employees. The lack of any further information should not be interpreted as either a favorable or unfavorable reference.

Submitted by:_____   Title:_____

Company: _____   Date: _____

REFUSAL TO GRANT REFERENCES

Date:

To:

Re:

     We have received your request for an employment reference on the above named individual, who was previously employed by us.

     While we would like to help you evaluate prospective employees, we regret that we cannot furnish you the requested information. It is our policy to limit information to the dates of employment, which we have completed below.

     We hope you understand the reasons for our policy.

Sincerely,

_____

     This confirms the above individual was employed by our company in the position of   between the dates of   , 19   , and   , 19   .

NOTICE OF CONFIDENTIALITY AGREEMENT

Date:

To:

Re:

     It has come to our attention that the above-named individual, whom we previously employed, is now employed by your organization.

     We wish to notify you of certain continuing obligations that said individual has to our company concerning confidential trade secrets and other proprietary information that may have been acquired or developed during this individual's employ with our company.

     It is not our intention to prevent this individual, nor any other former employee, from using the general knowledge of the industry or skills acquired while employed by our company. Protecting our company's confidential information is our only concern. As a business organization also possessing confidential data and trade secrets, you can appreciate our position, I am sure. Your cooperation in this matter will be greatly appreciated.

     For informational purposes, I am also sending a copy of this letter to:

Sincerely,

_____

COBRA LETTER TO TERMINATING EMPLOYEE

Date:

To:

Dear   :

You are eligible to receive health care coverage from our company as a result of the Consolidated Omnibus Budget Reconciliation Act (COBRA).

This regulation affects former employees, including retirees and dependents of employees, whose coverage under our health care program has stopped.

Under this law, you may purchase the same medical, dental, and prescription drug coverage provided to current employees for up to 18 months. The attached sheet summarizes the items covered by the medical plan.

Your monthly cost is $ for individual coverage and $ for family coverage. This is equal to the company's cost of providing the same coverage to each of our current employees. You are not required to furnish proof of insurability to receive this coverage.

To accept the coverage, complete and sign the enclosed application form and mail it to our Personnel Department within 60 days of receipt of this letter. The premium may be paid monthly or in a single payment and is due within 45 days of your application for coverage. Payments should also be mailed to the Personnel Department.

Benefits under this program stop automatically at the end of the 18-month period, or sooner if you stop making the payments, become covered under another employer's health care plan, or become eligible for Medicare. Benefits could also stop if for some reason our company discontinued the employee health care plan.

If you fail to apply for coverage within 60 days, or fail to send your first premium payment within 45 days of enrolling, you forfeit your right to coverage under the plan.

If you have any questions about the program, please call me at_____.

Sincerely,

_____
Personnel Manager

COBRA EMPLOYEE INFORMATION LETTER

Date:

To:

Dear   :

    Under the provisions of the Consolidated Omnibus Budget Reconciliation Act of 1985 (COBRA), you may elect to continue your Major Medical and dental coverage at group rates through   for a period of up to 18 months.

    If you elect to do so, you must reimburse the company each month for no more than 102% of actual costs, the 2% being an administration fee allowed by law.

    The present rates are as follows. However, these rates may change. If they do, you will be advised via changes to your monthly invoice. Payment is due on the   day of each month.

	Medical	Continue? (Yes/No)
Single	$_____	_____
Husband/Wife	$_____	_____
Family	$_____	_____
	Dental	
Single	$_____	_____
Family	$_____	_____

Please advise us of your decision (whether yes or no) as soon as possible by returning the enclosed copy of this letter. For your convenience, we have also enclosed a self-addressed stamped envelope.

                         Sincerely,

_____

_____Yes, I wish to continue my insurance on the above terms.

_____No, I do not wish to continue my insurance.

_____   _____
Supervisor   Date

COBRA COMPLIANCE

Employee: _____

Department: _____ Position: _____

Benefits Ending Dates:

        Employer   _____/_____/_____

        COBRA   _____/_____/_____

Date Employee Notified   _____/_____/_____

Employee: Accepted (   )   Rejected (   )   No Response (   )

Comments: _____

_____

_____

_____

_____
Signed